THE HISTORY OF CINDERELLA OR THE LITTLE GLASS SLIPPER

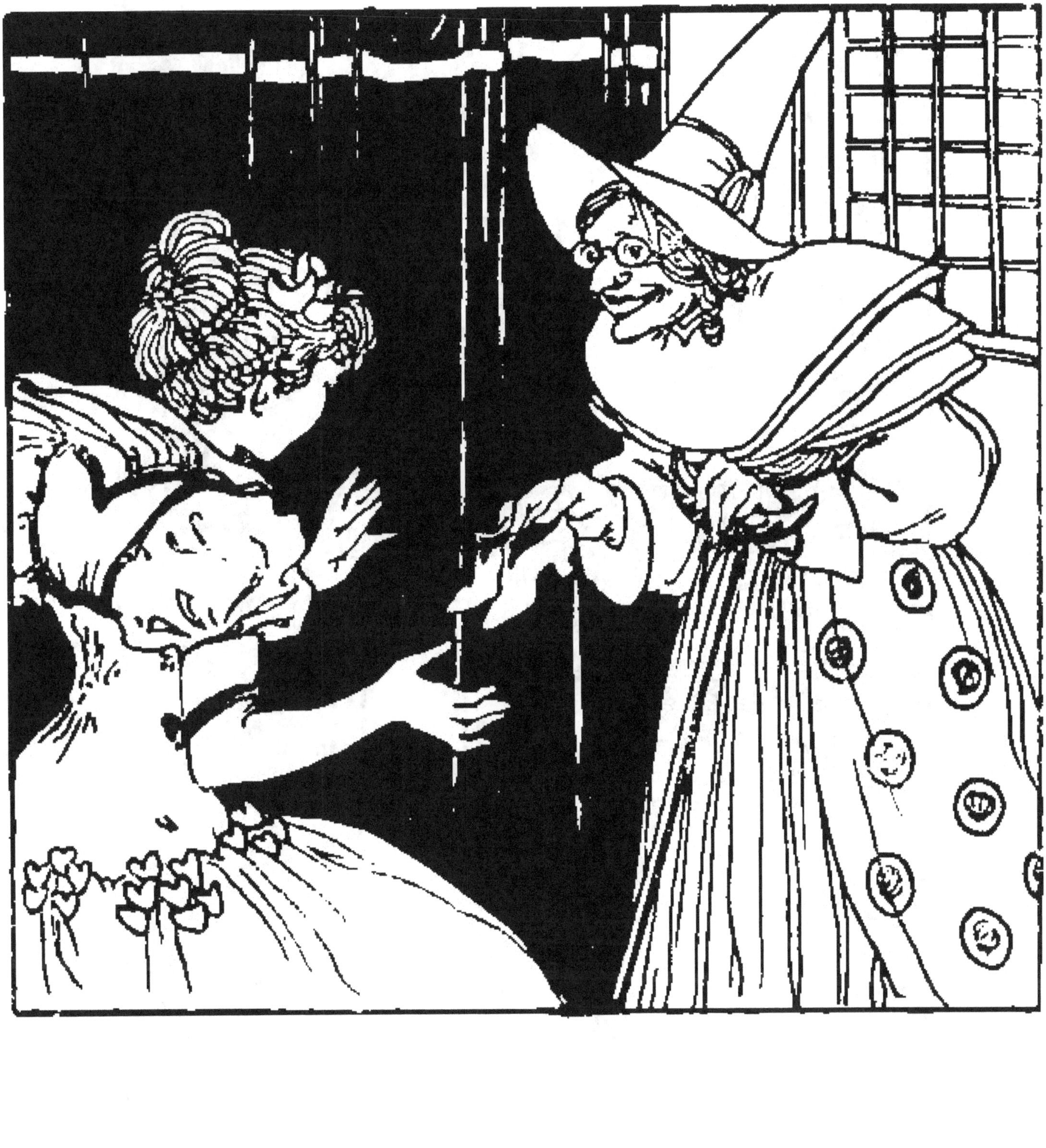

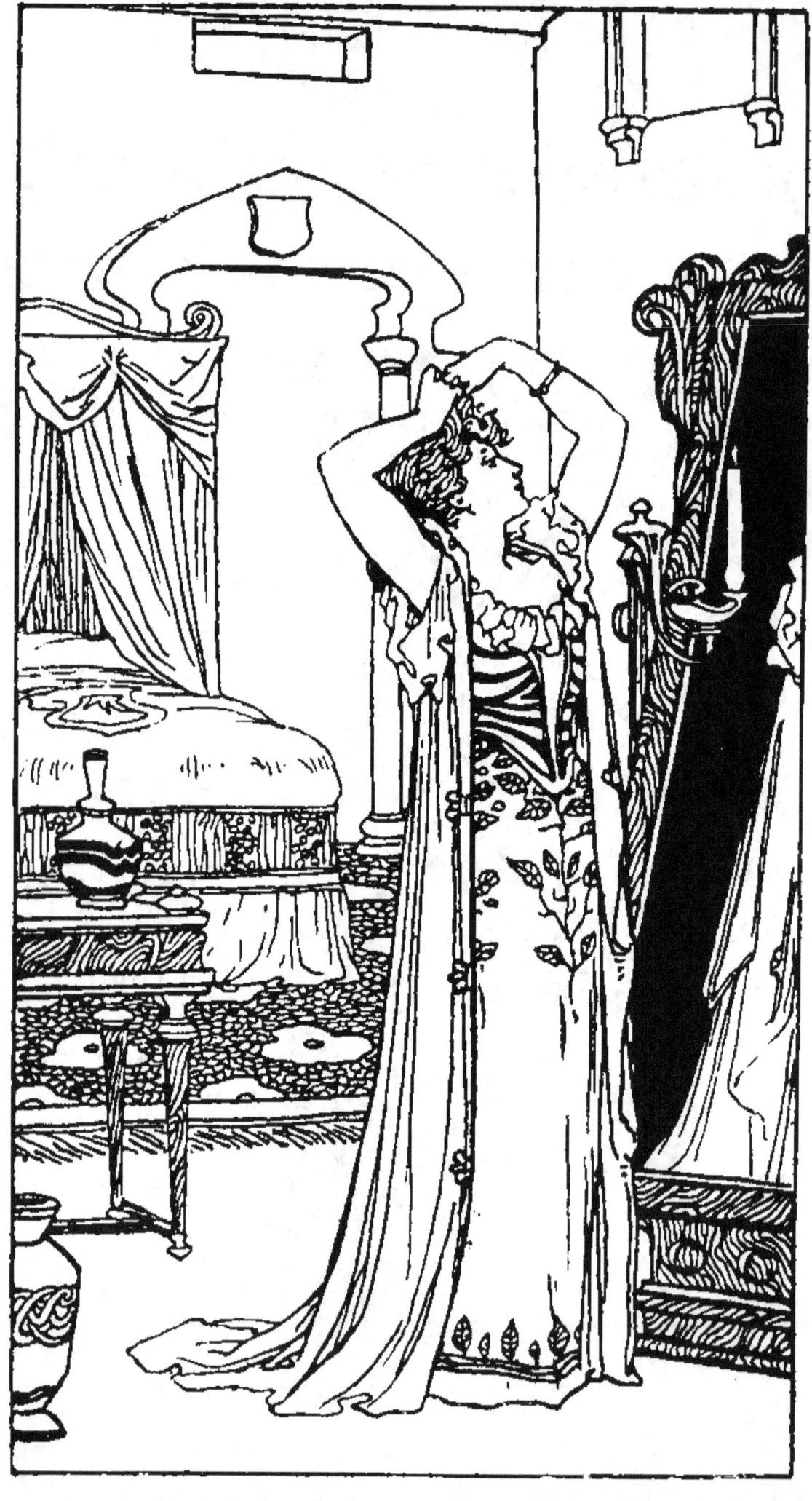

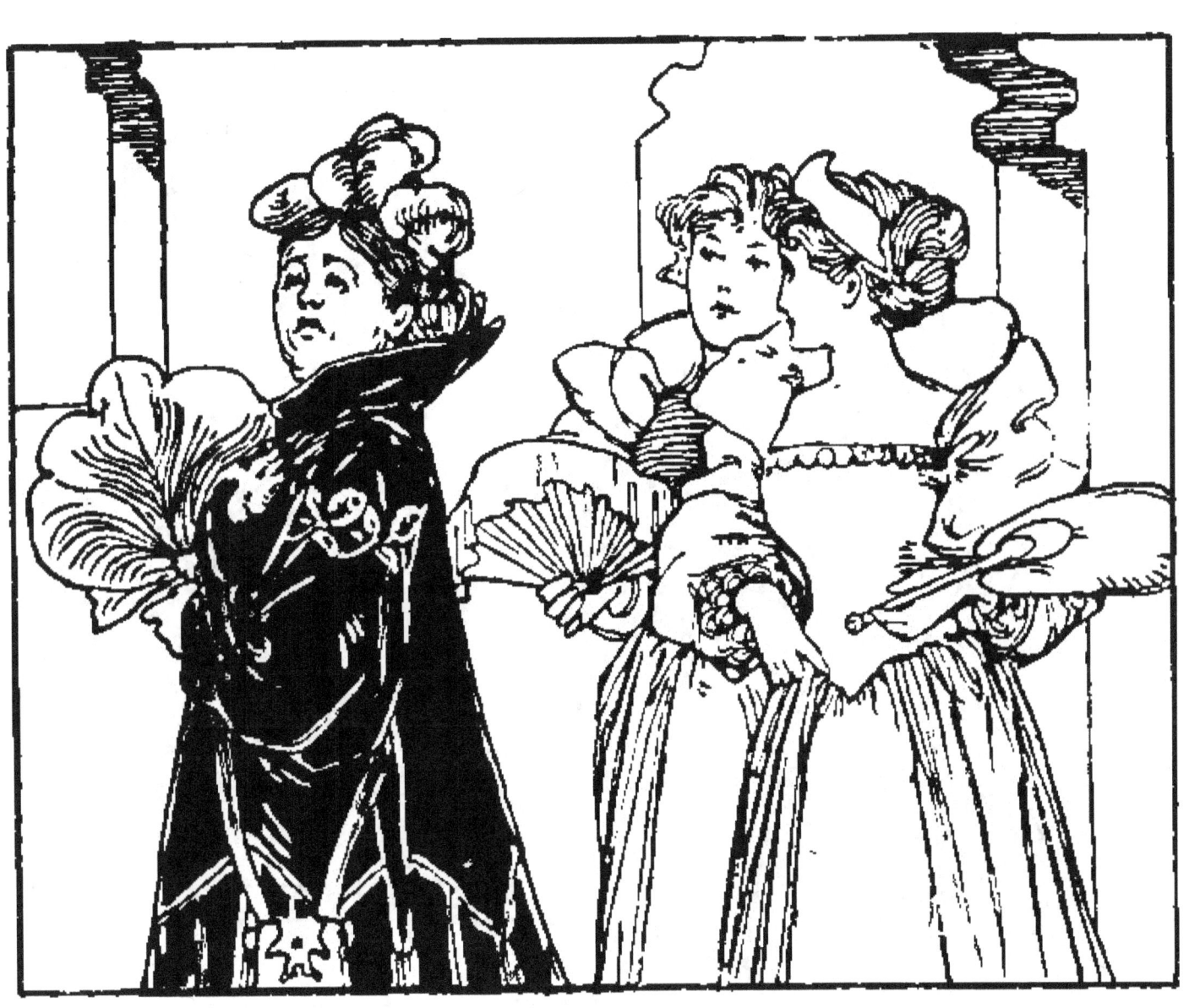

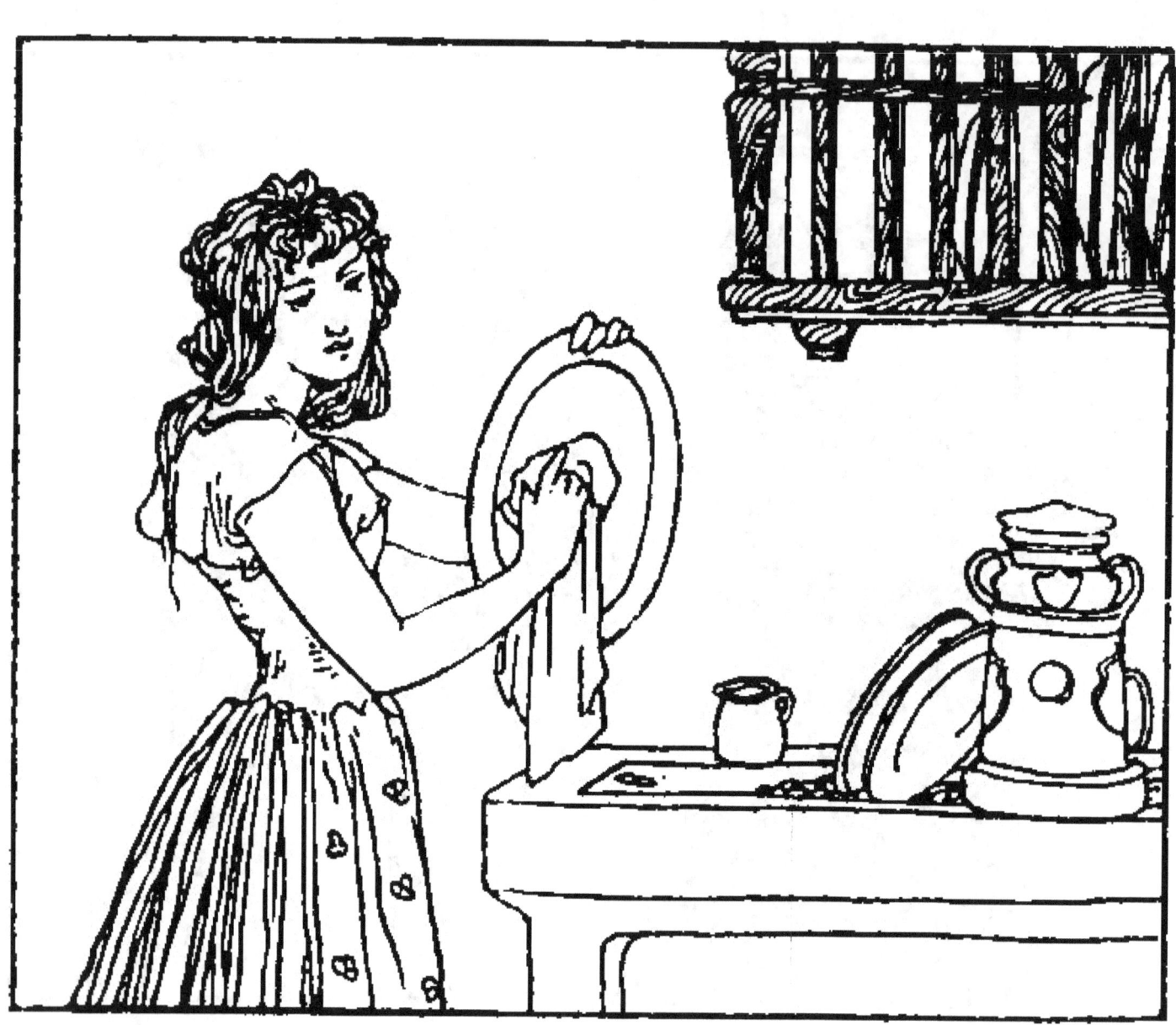

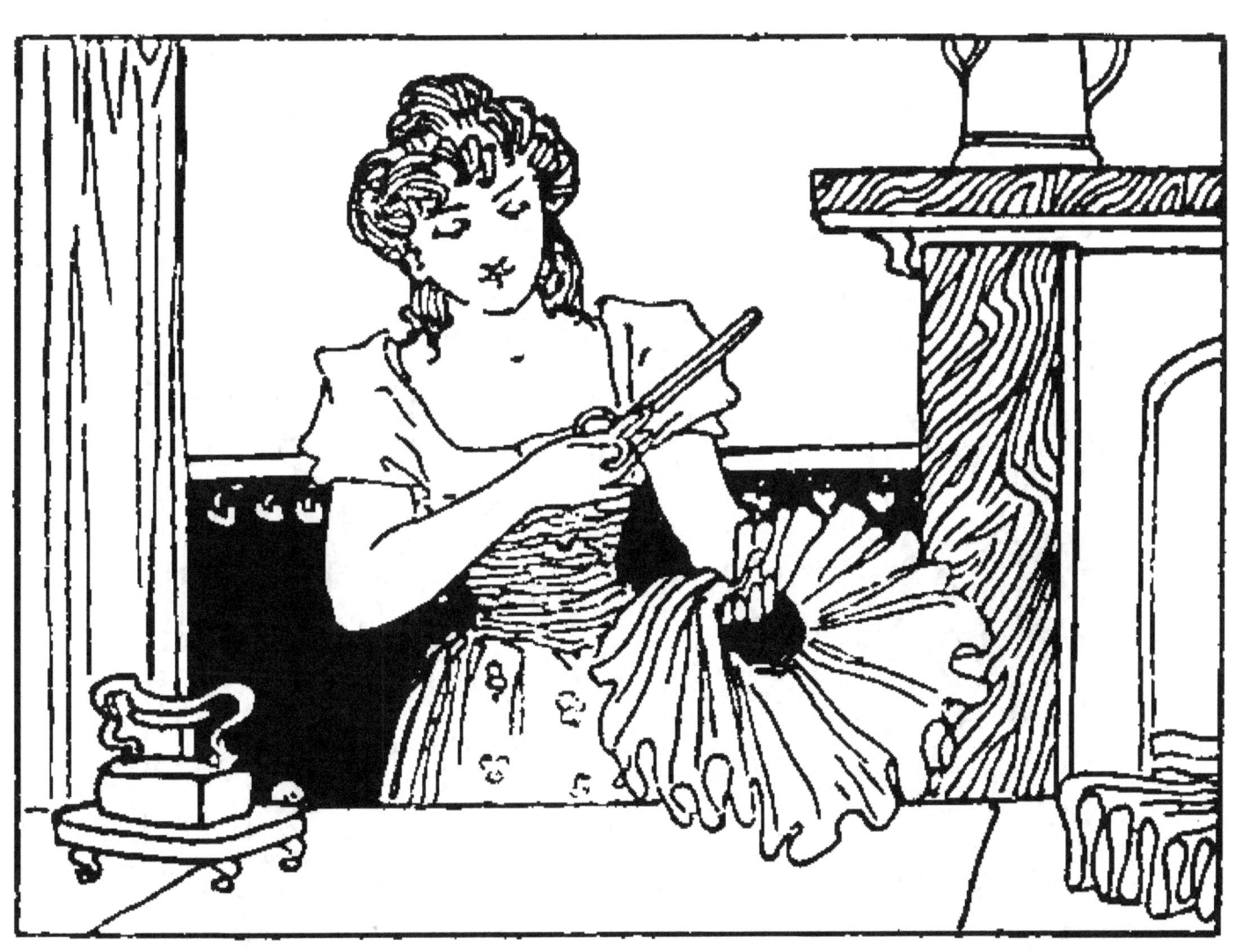

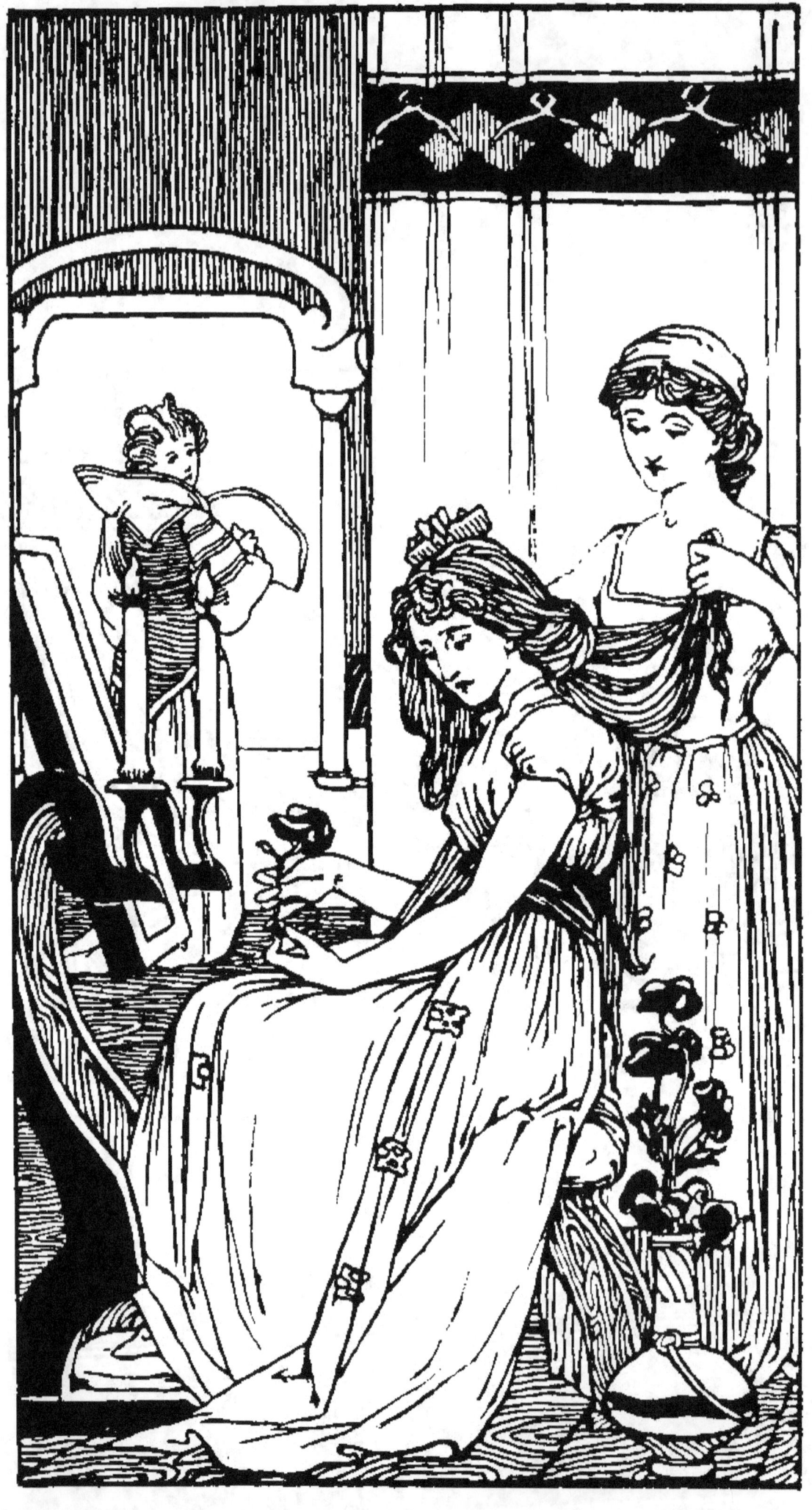

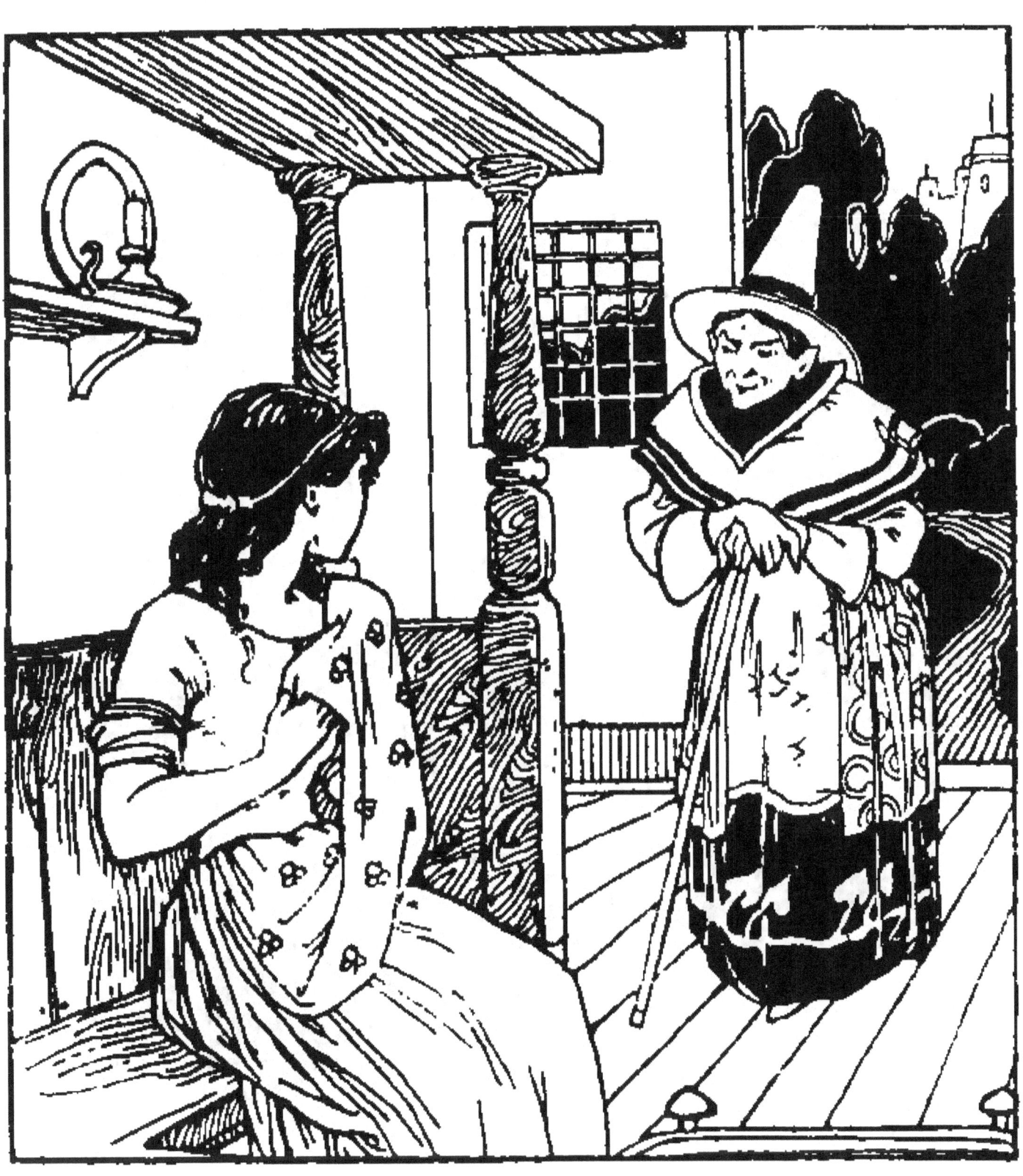

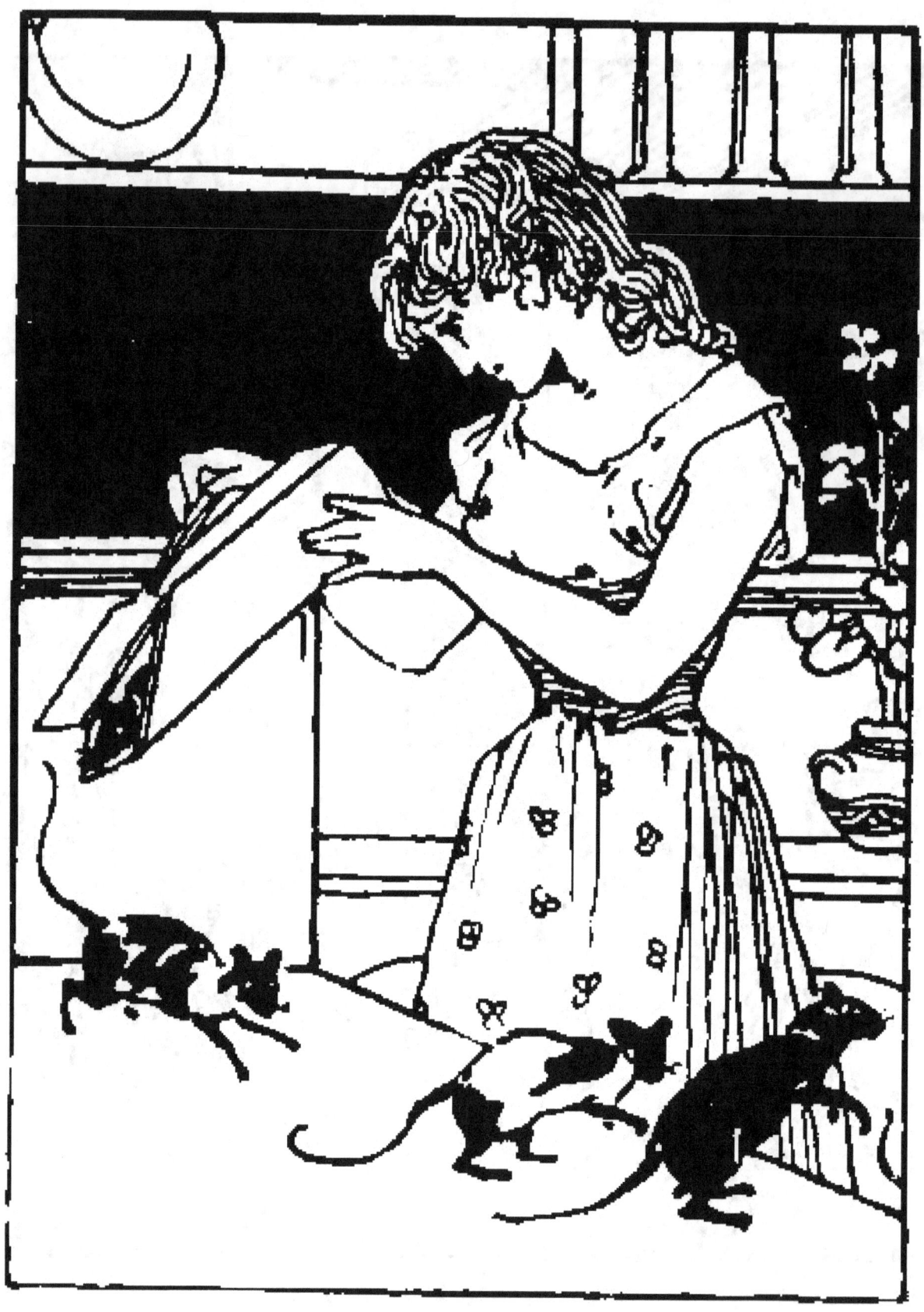

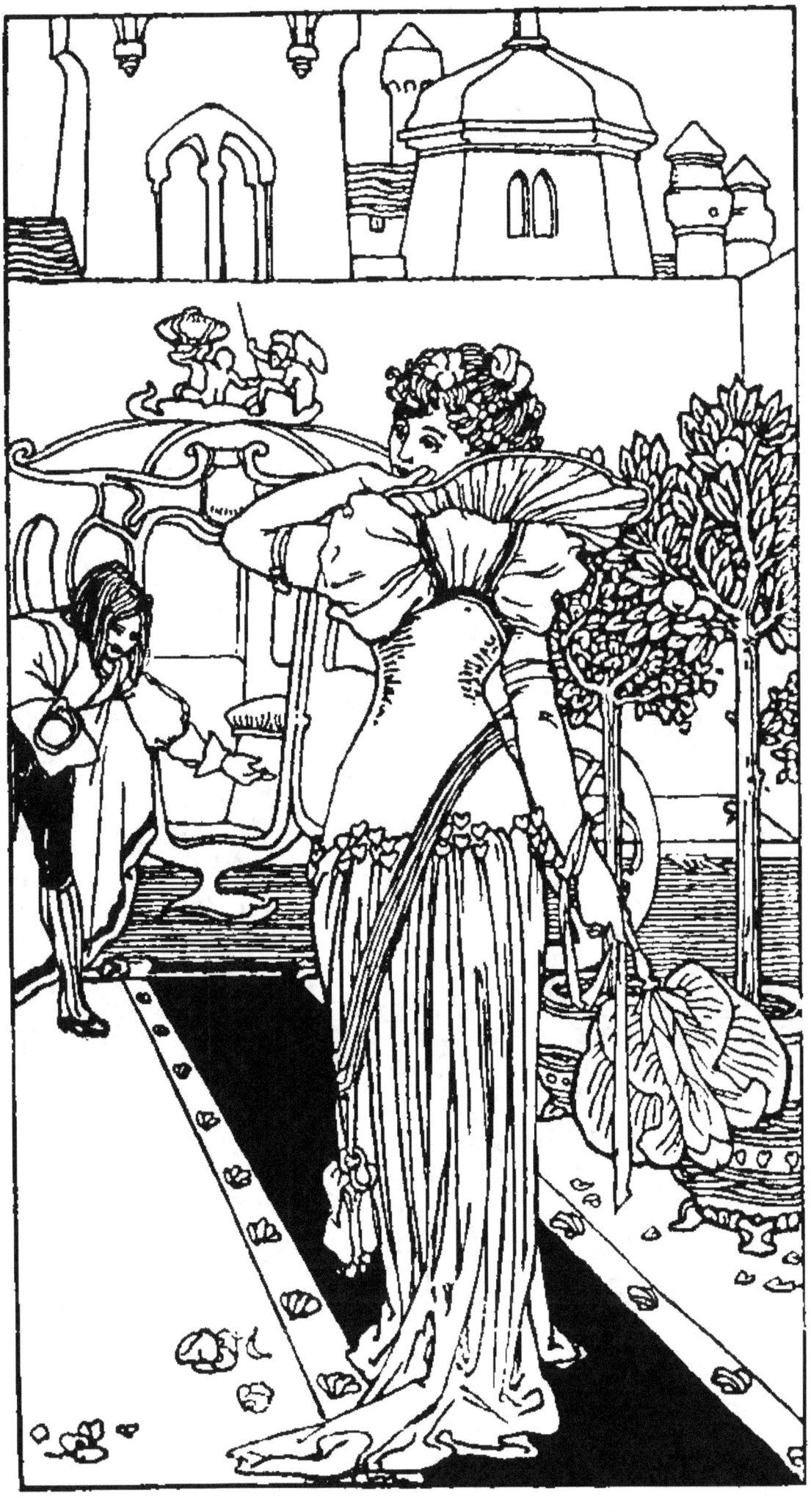

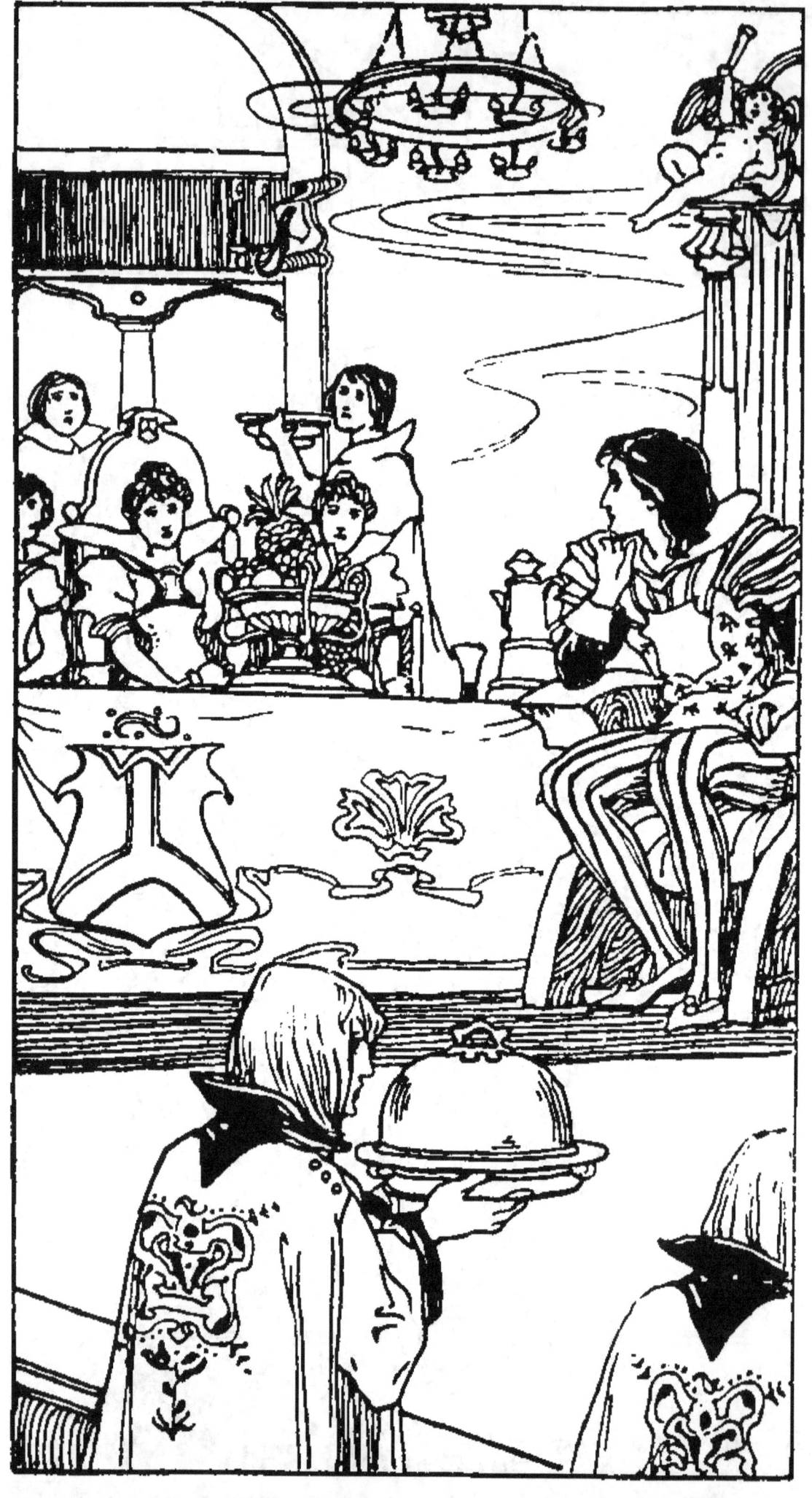

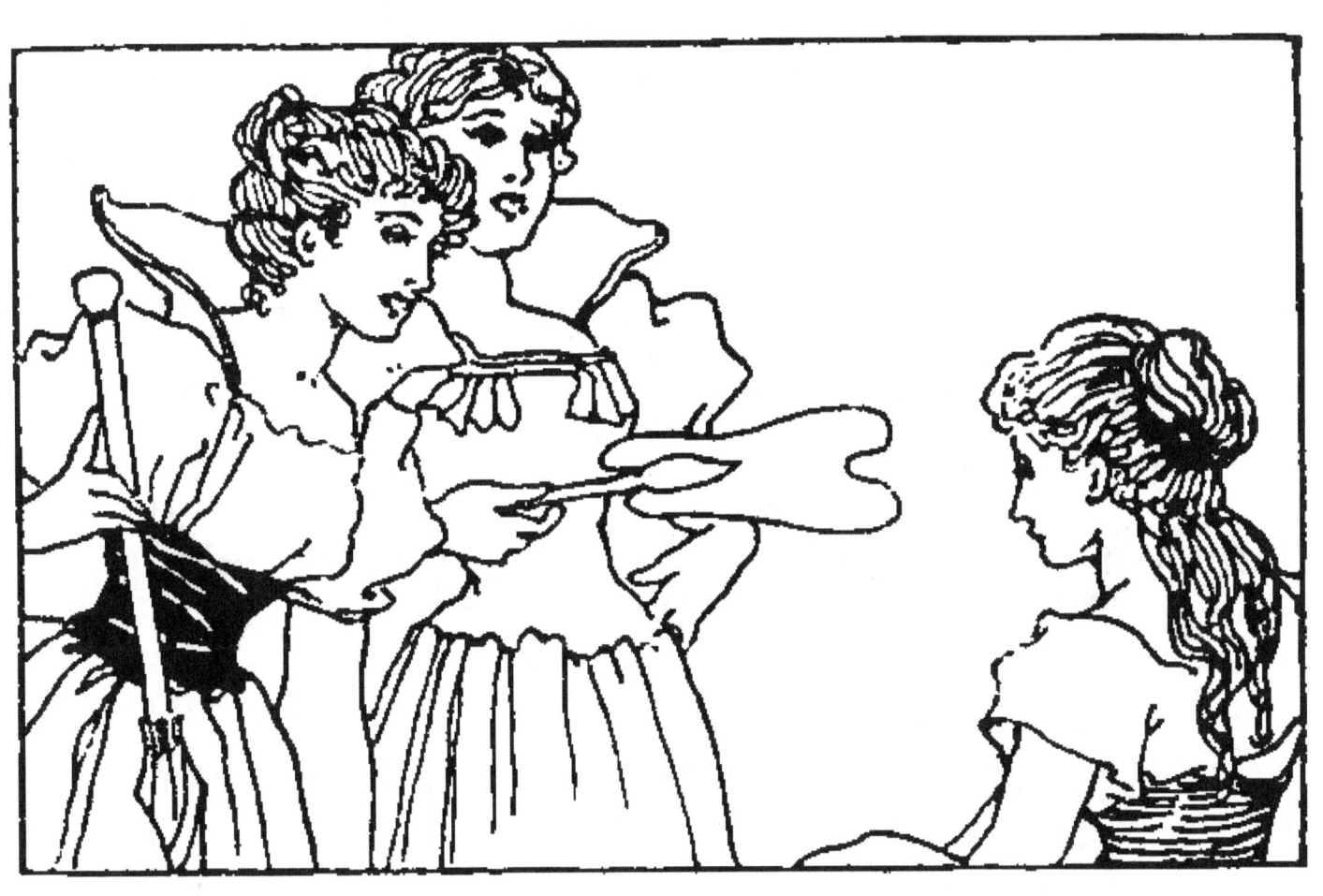

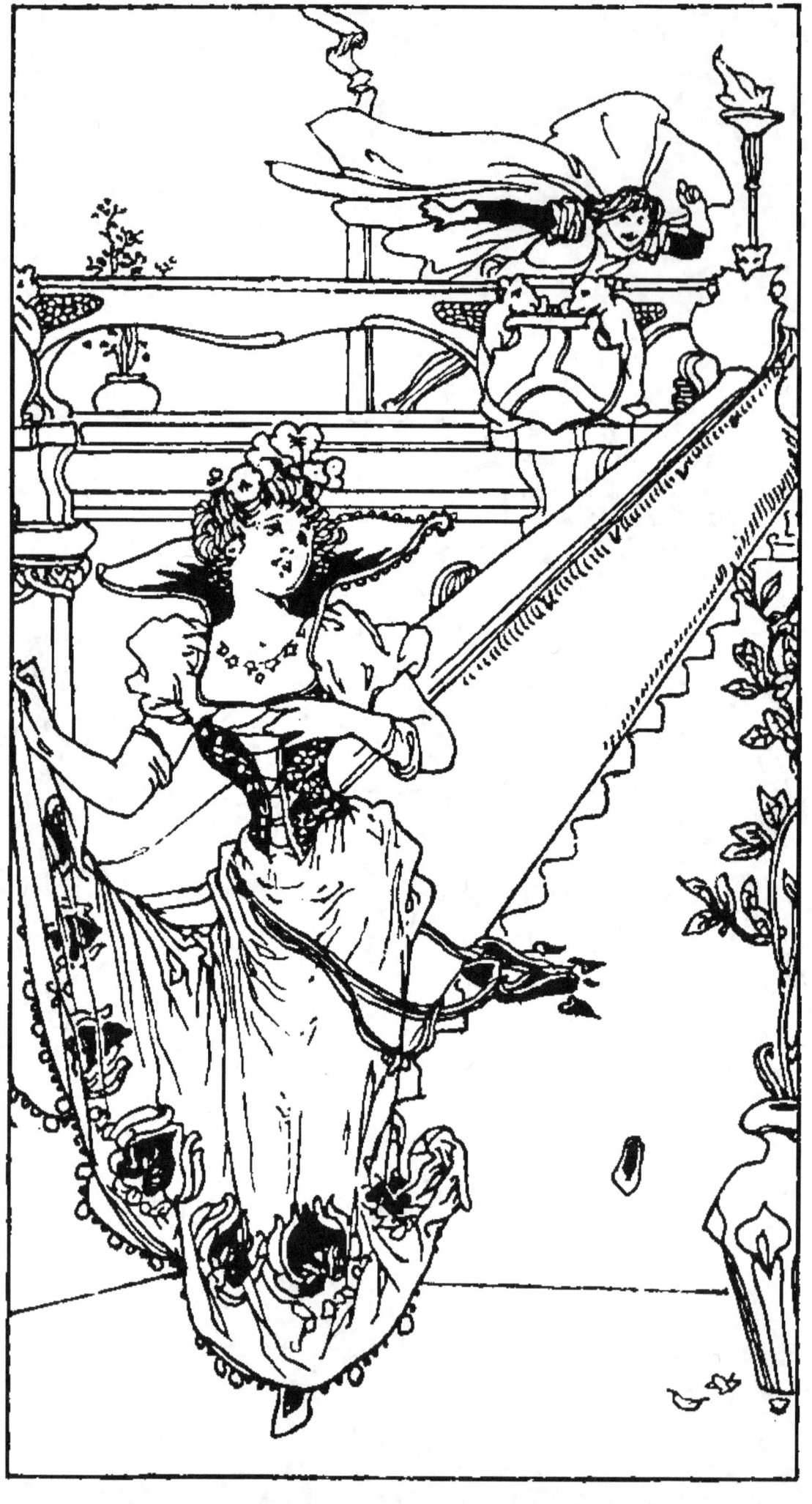

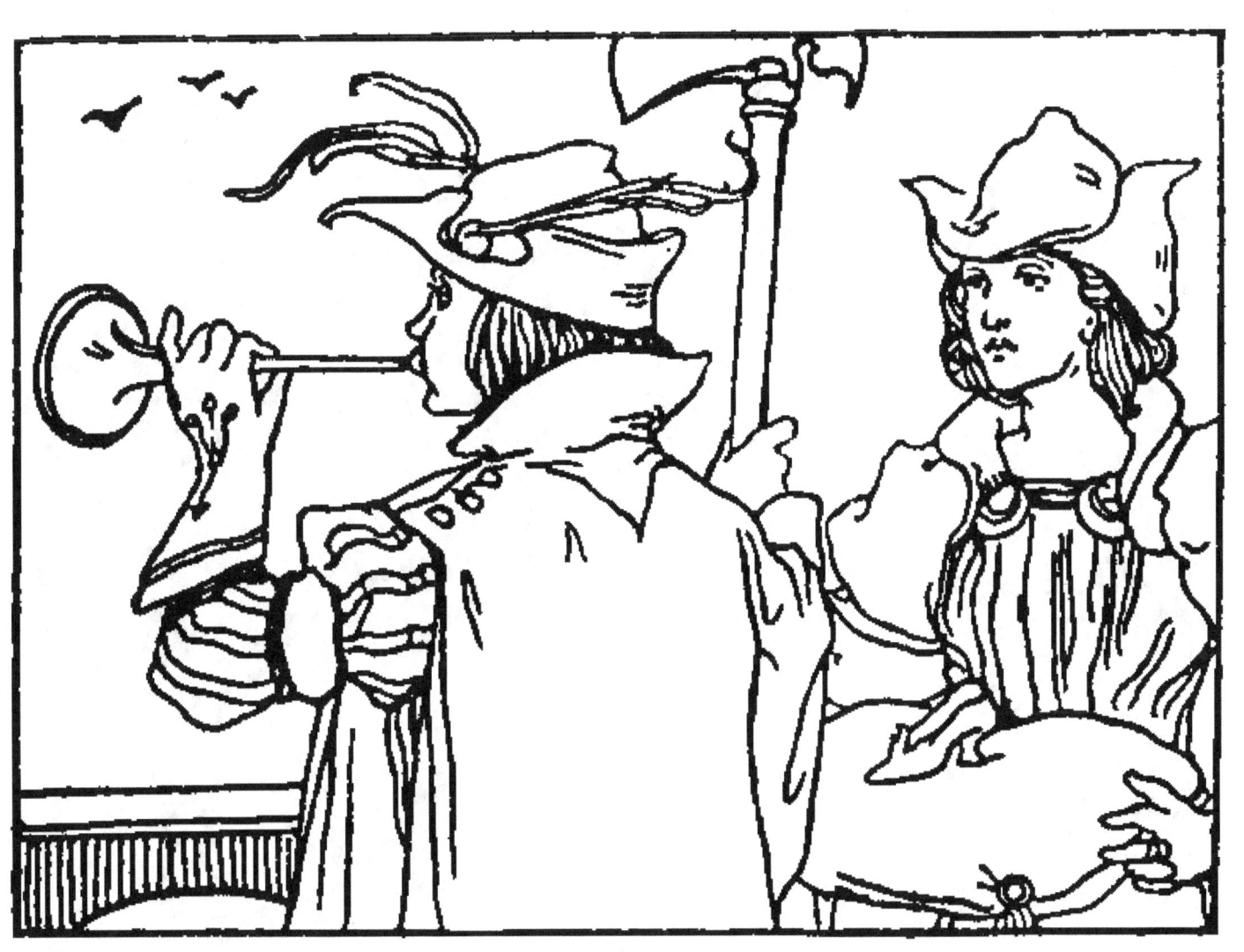

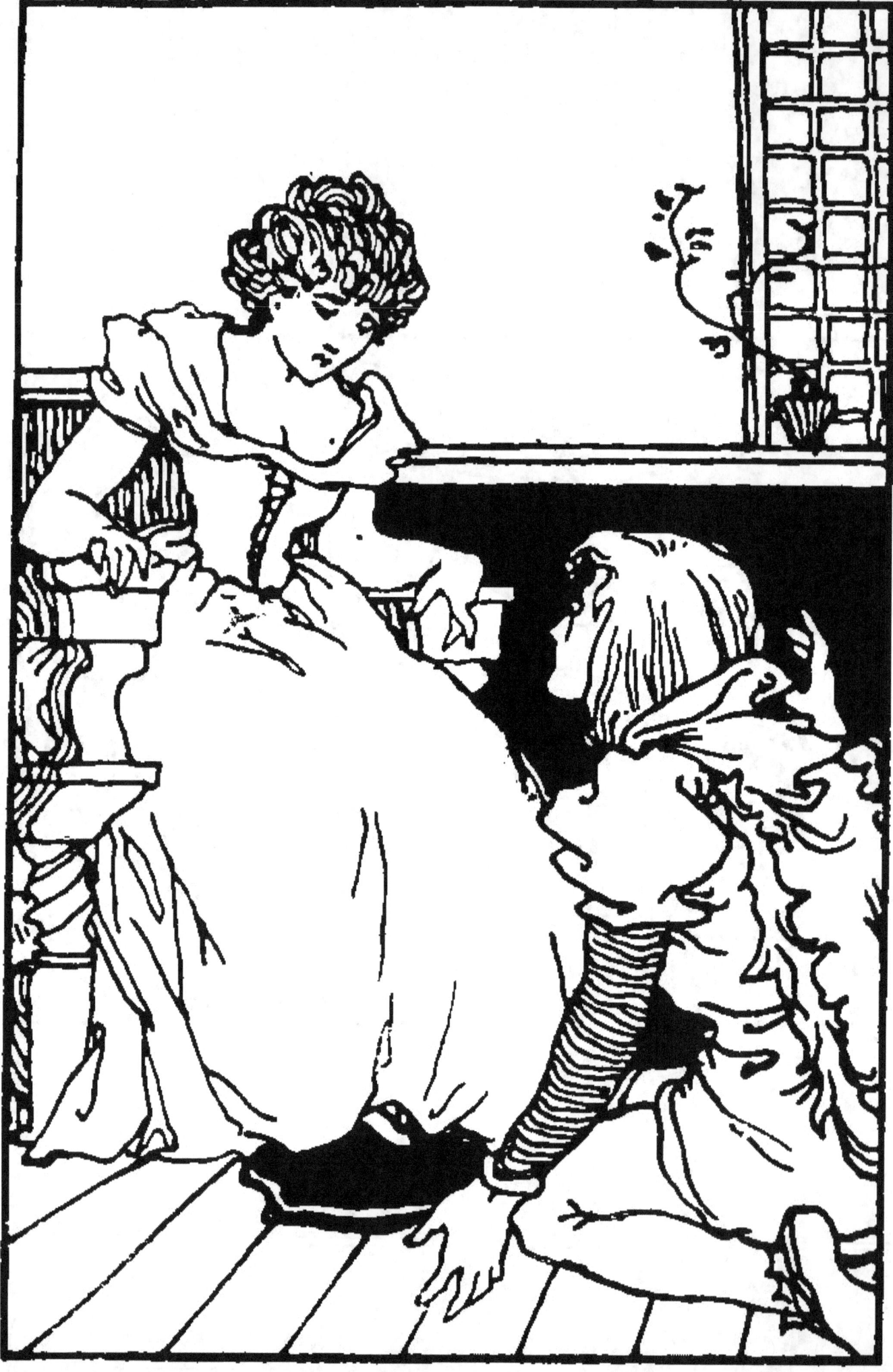

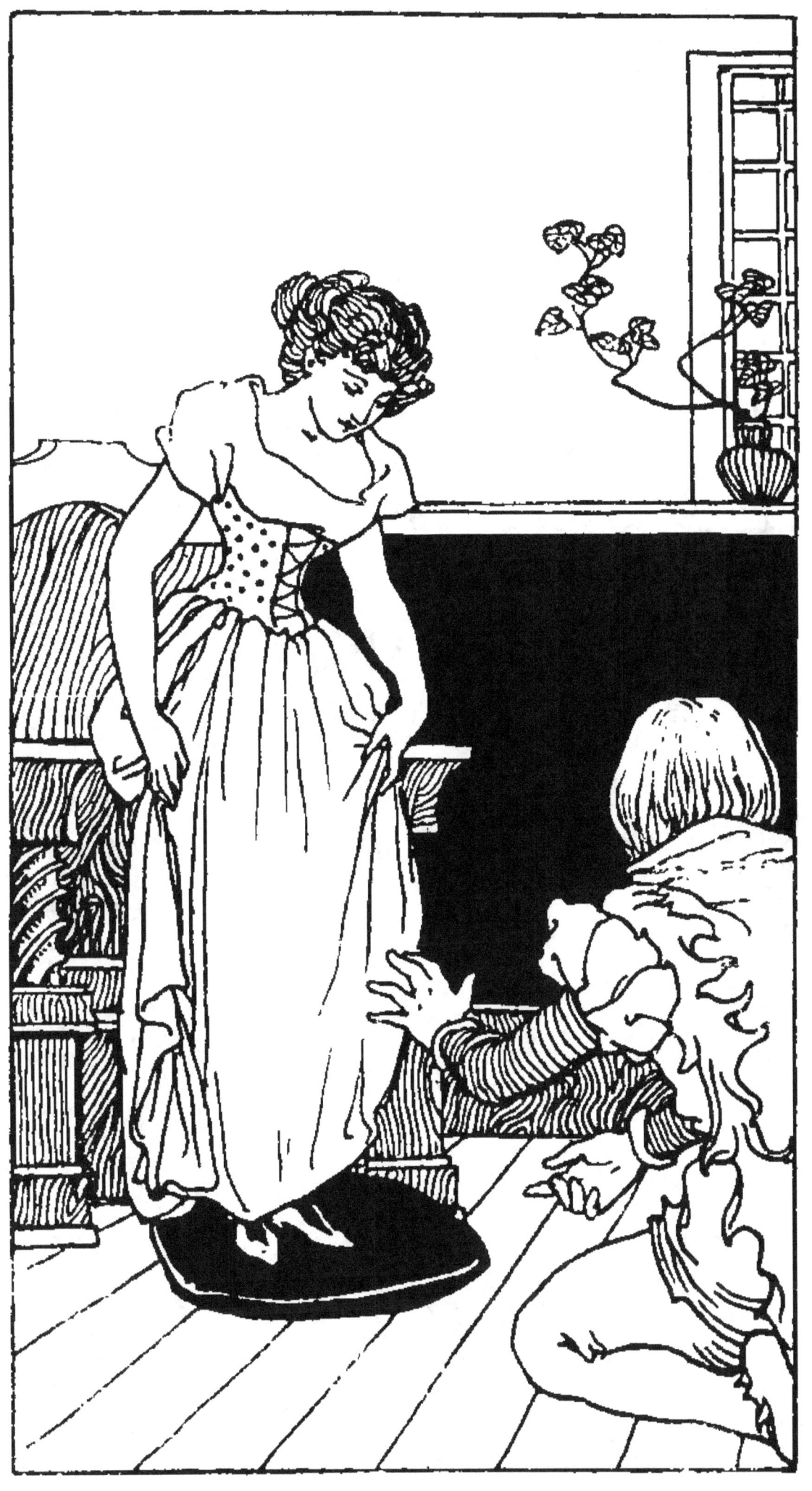

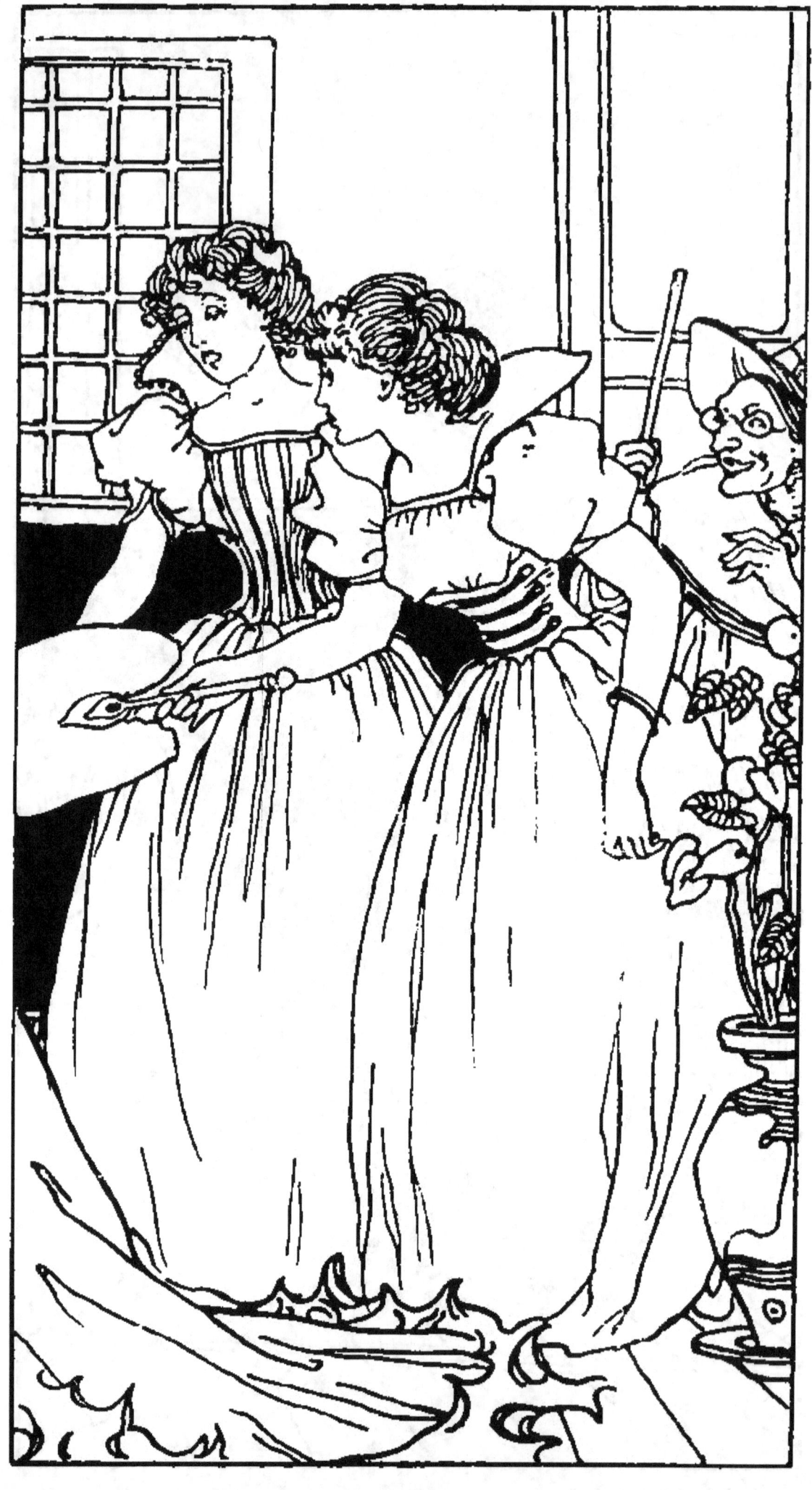

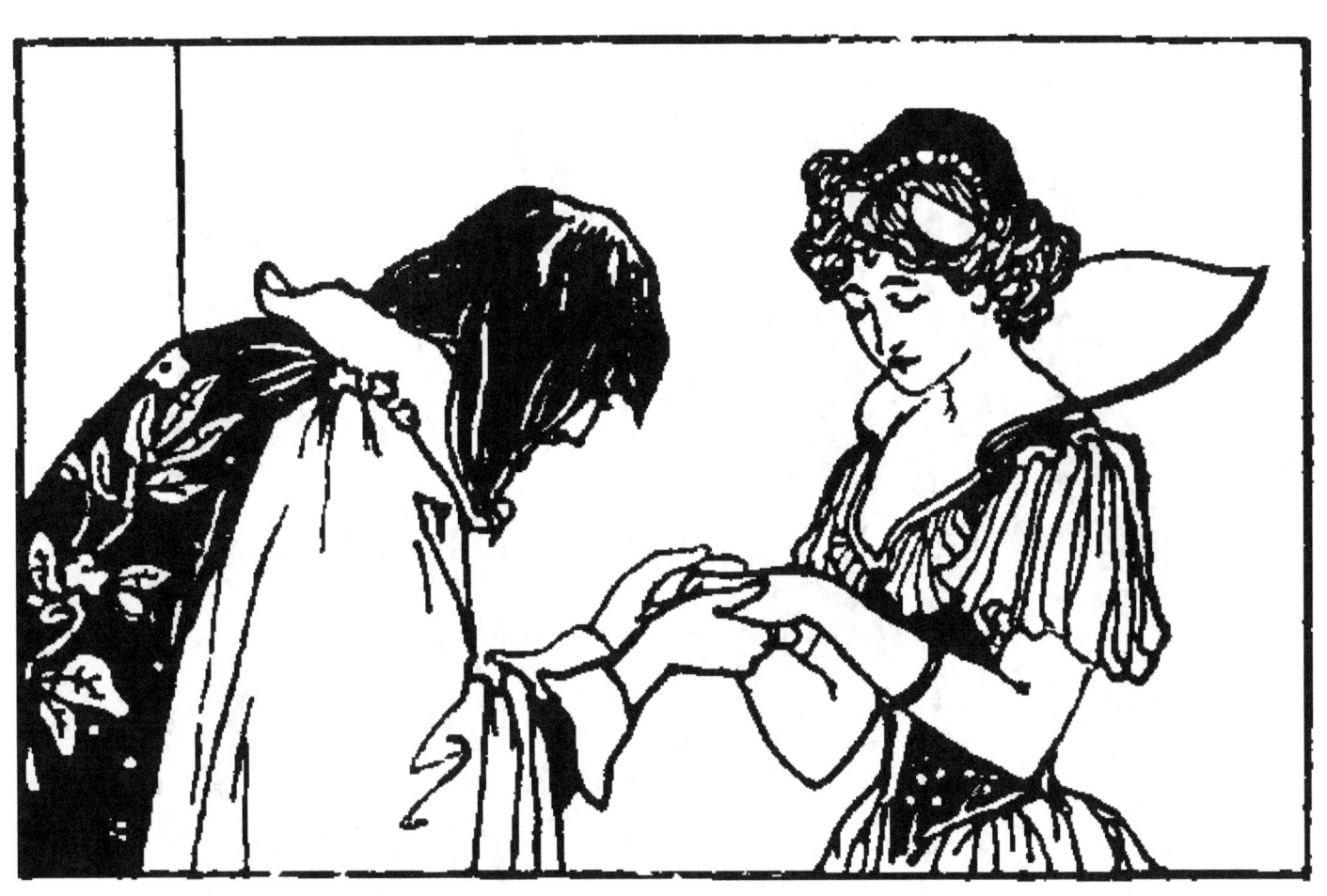

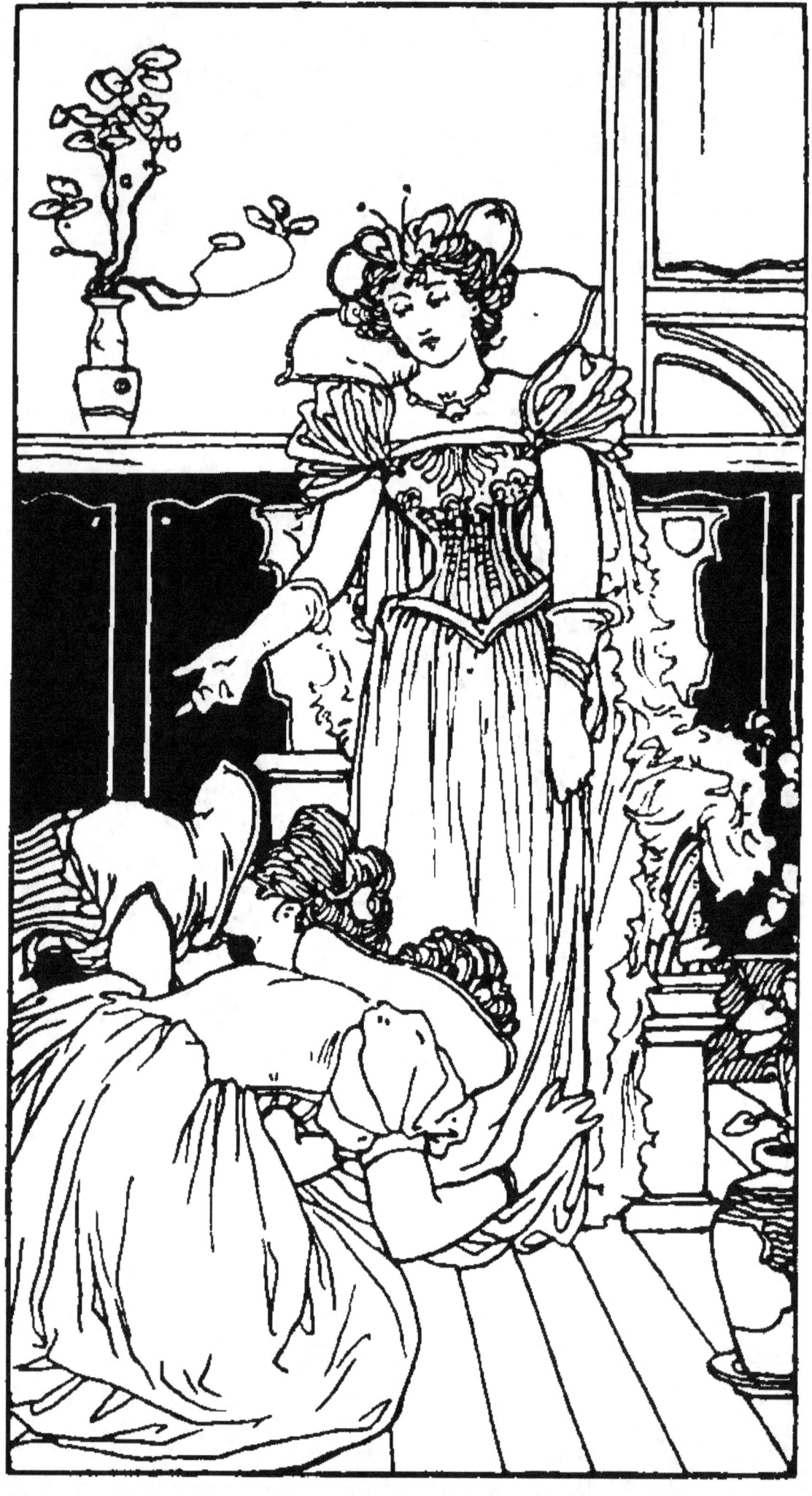

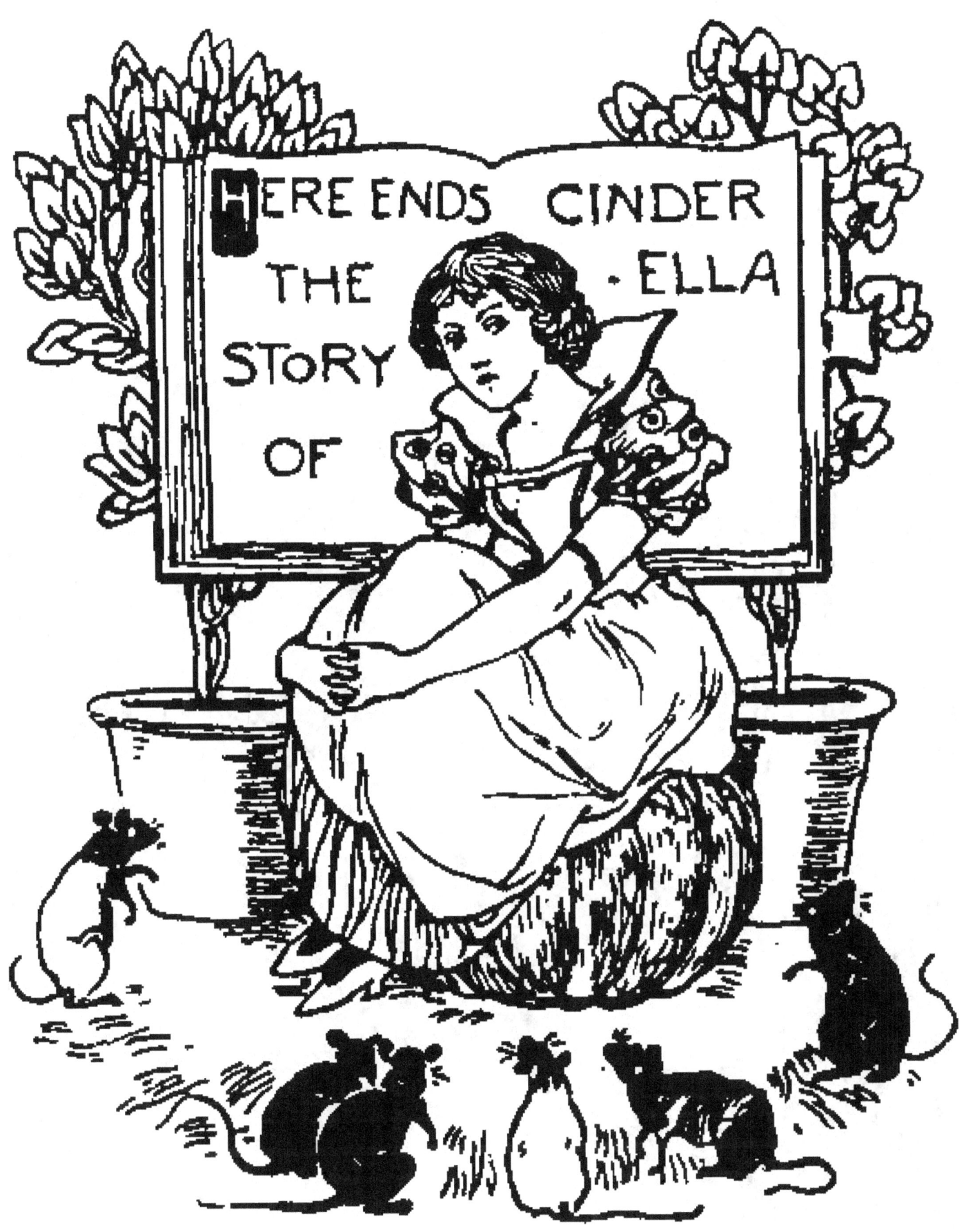

THE HISTORY OF JACK AND THE BEANSTALK.

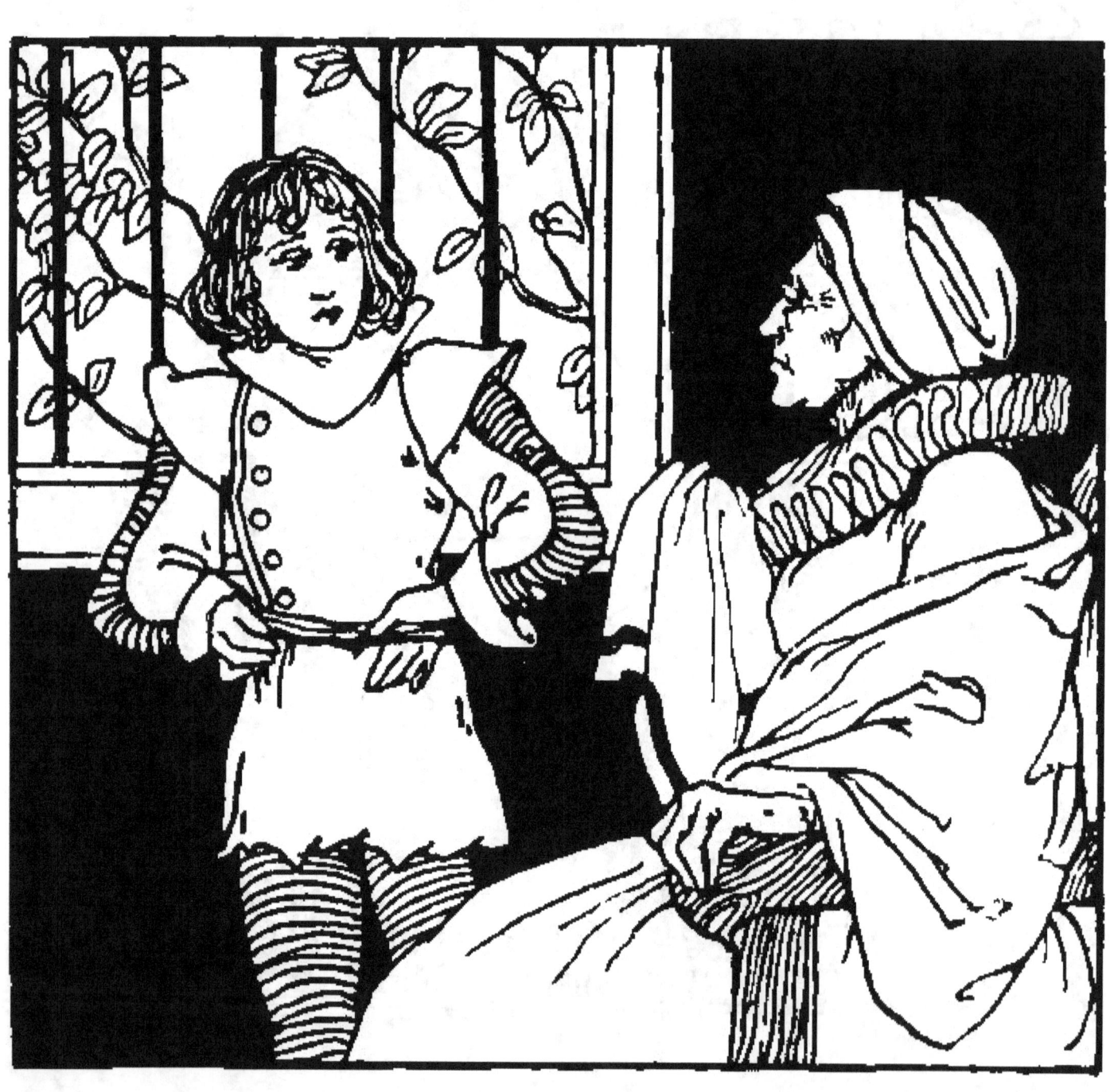

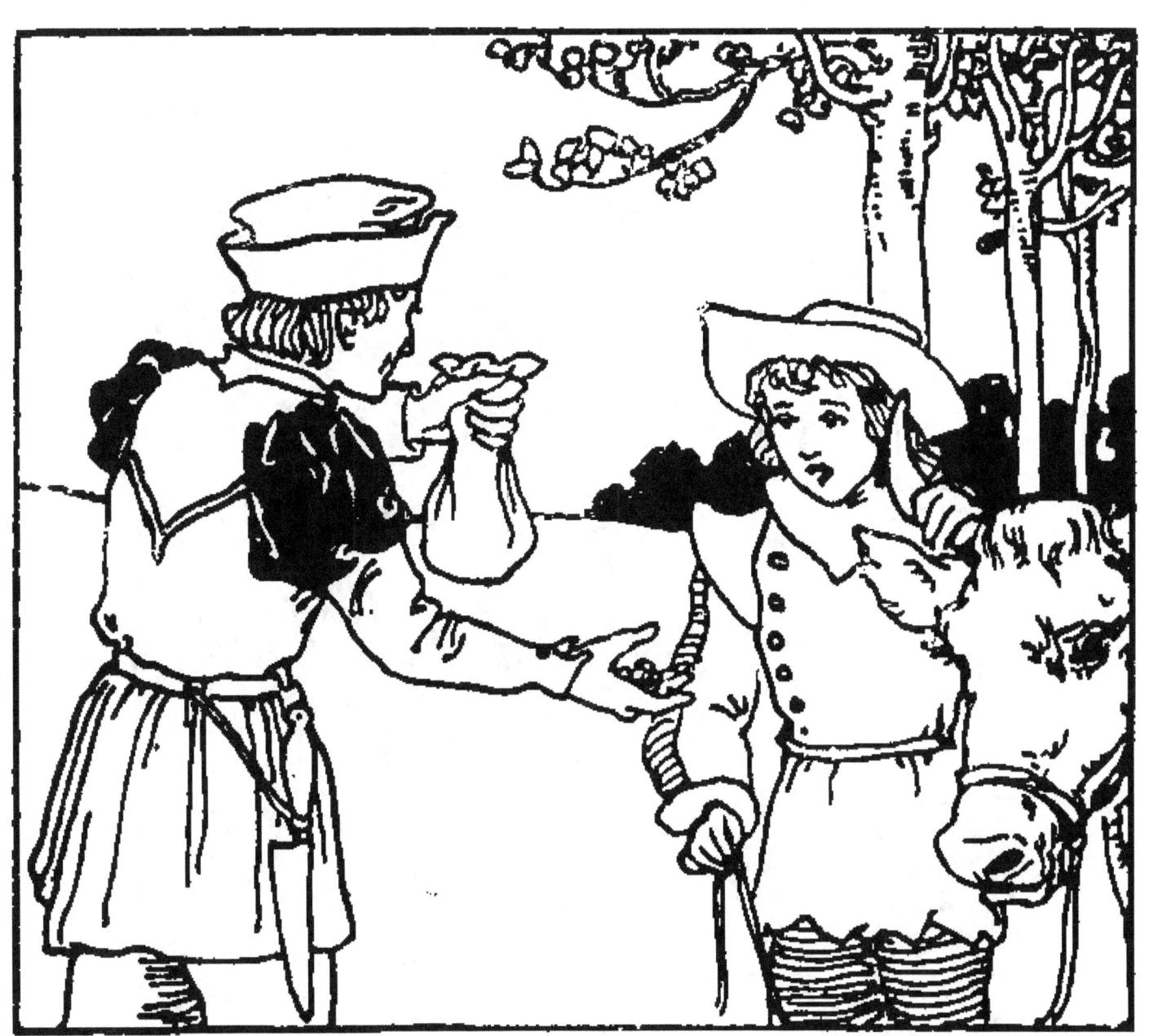

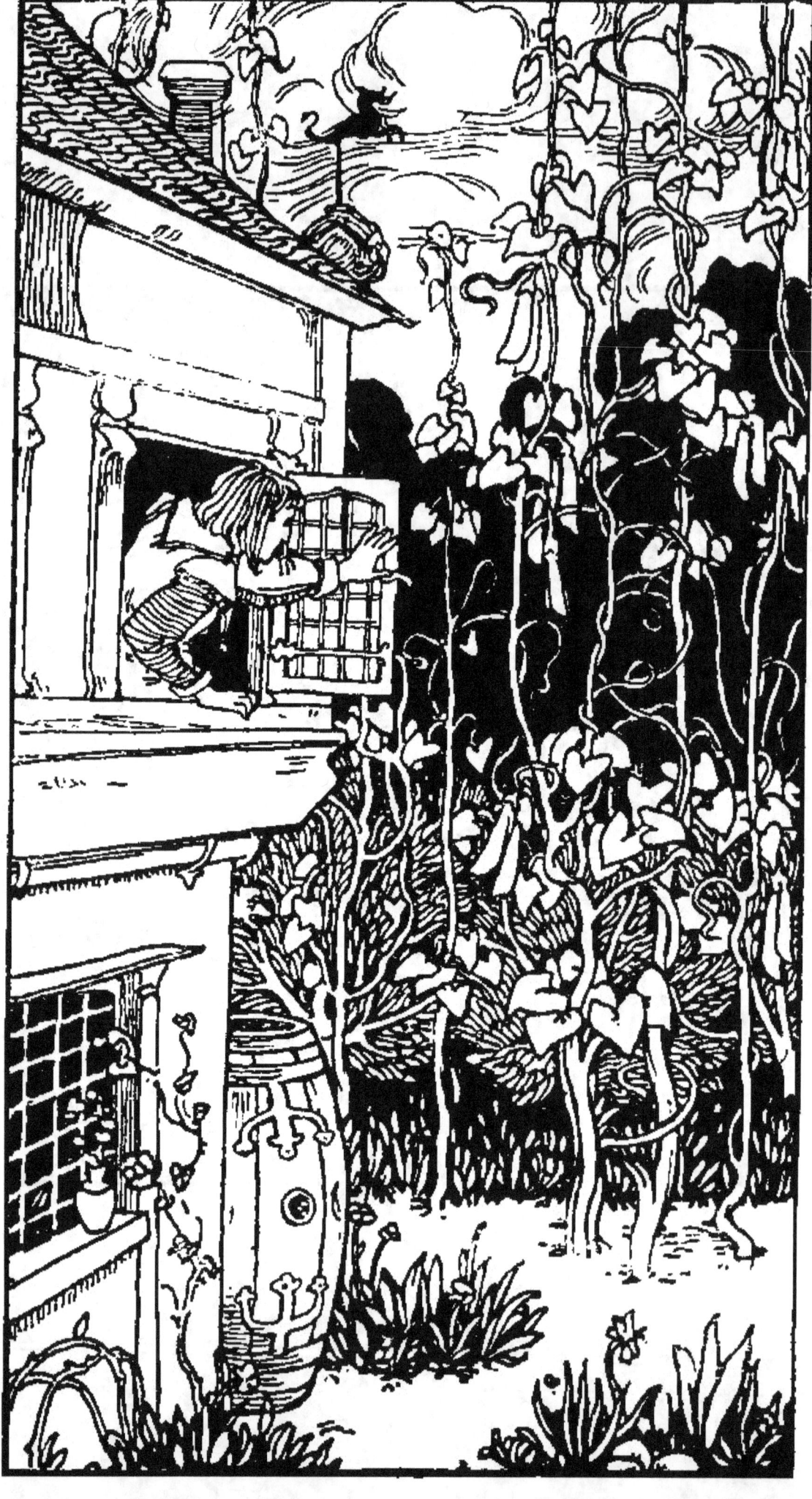

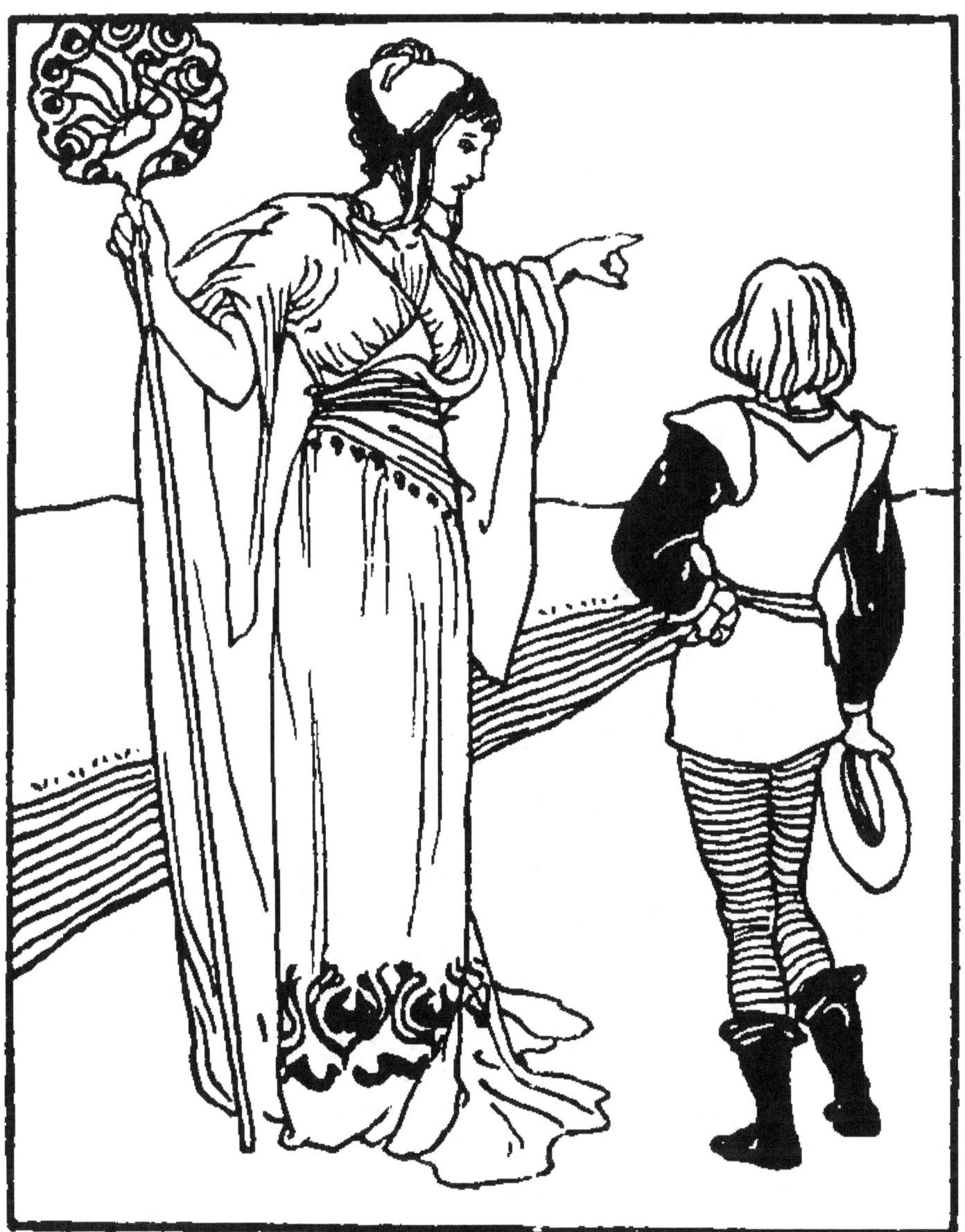

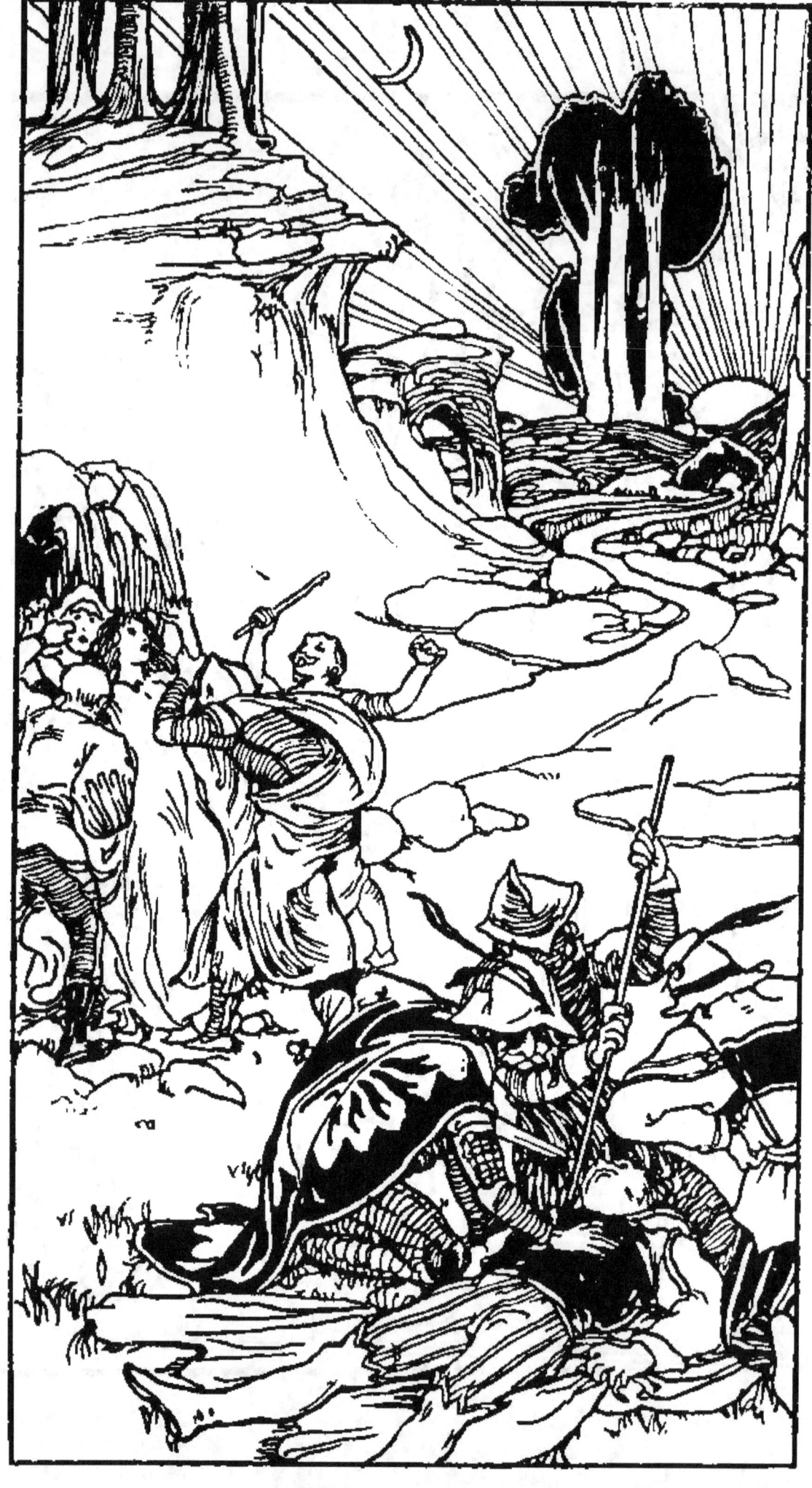

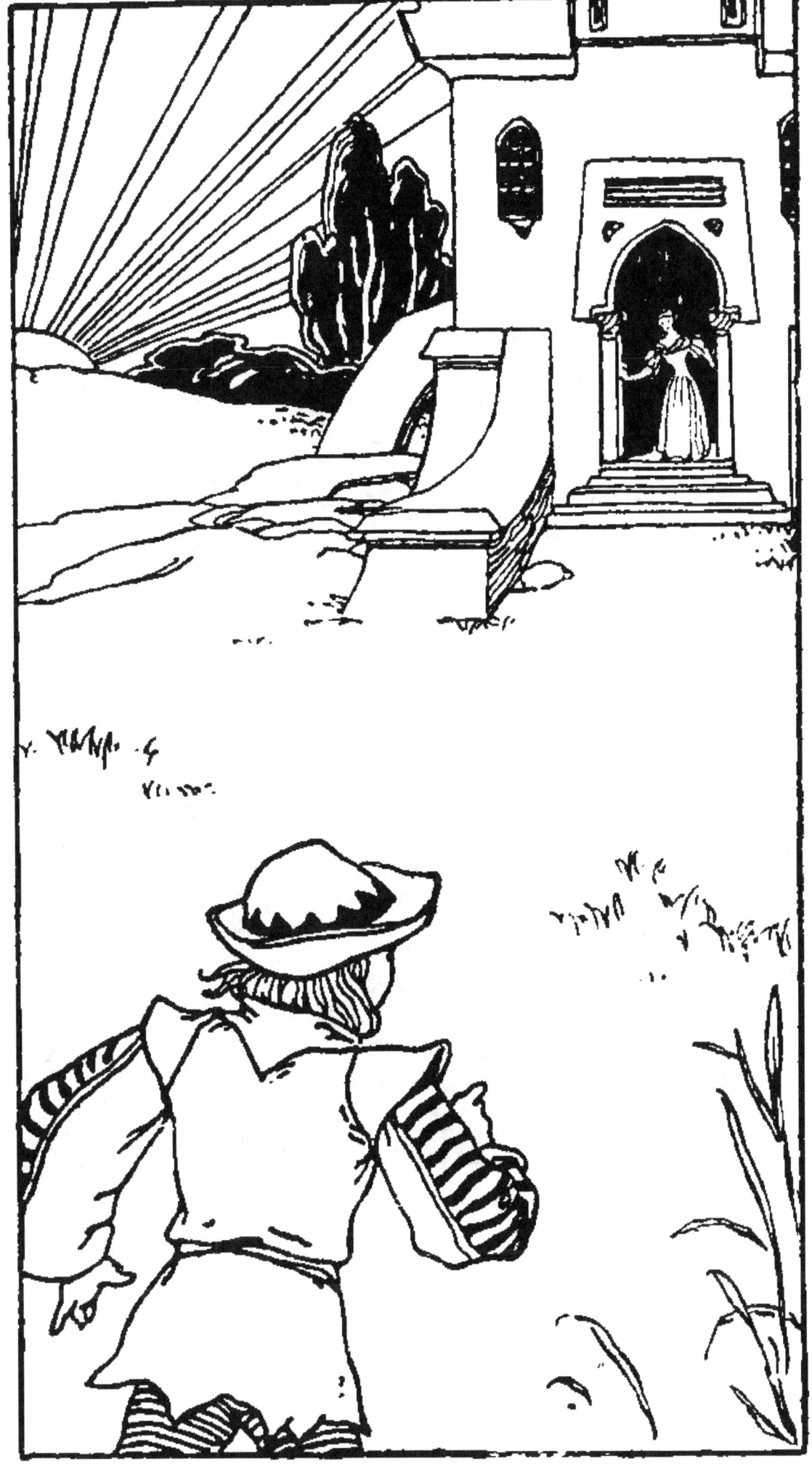

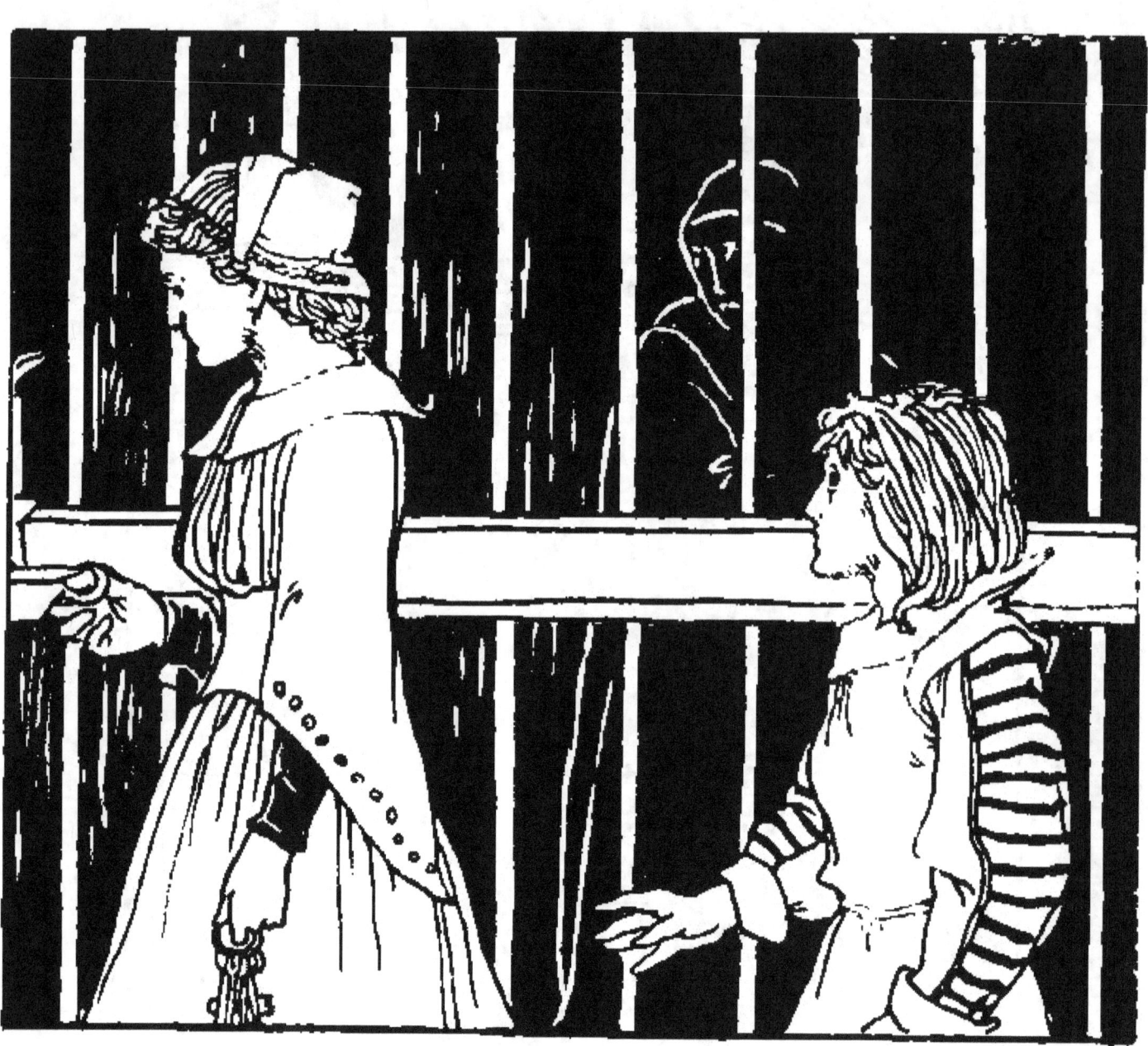

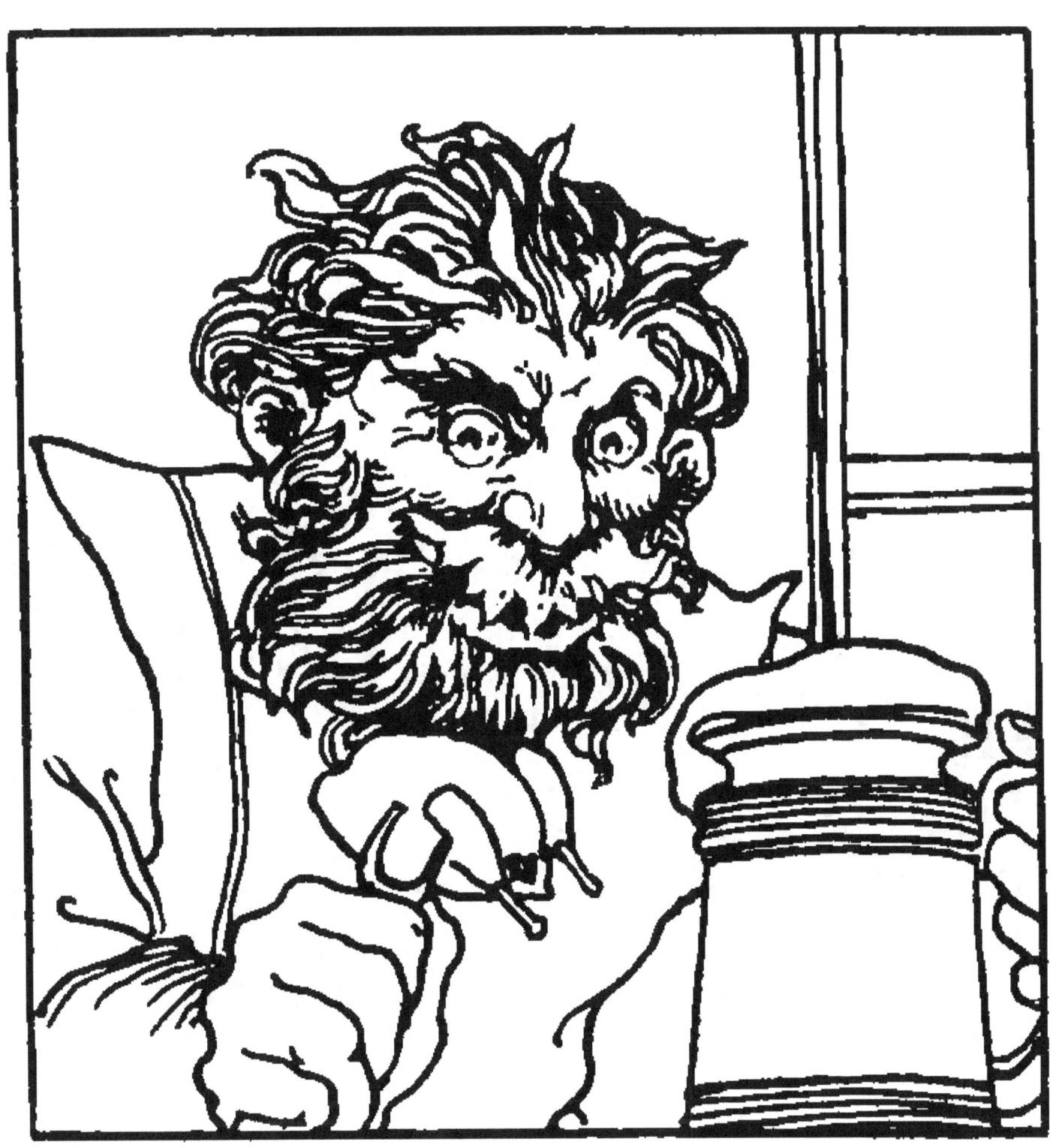

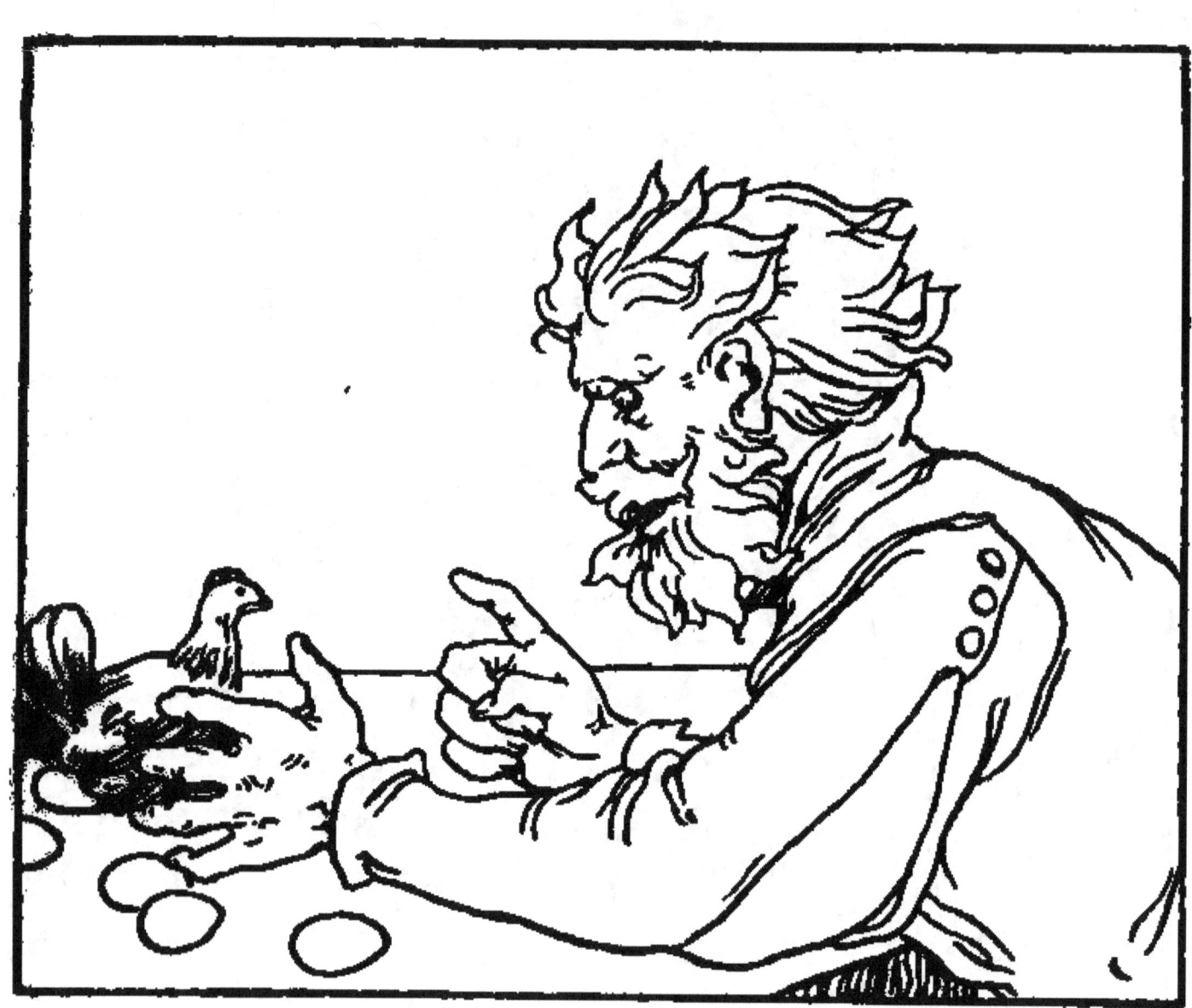

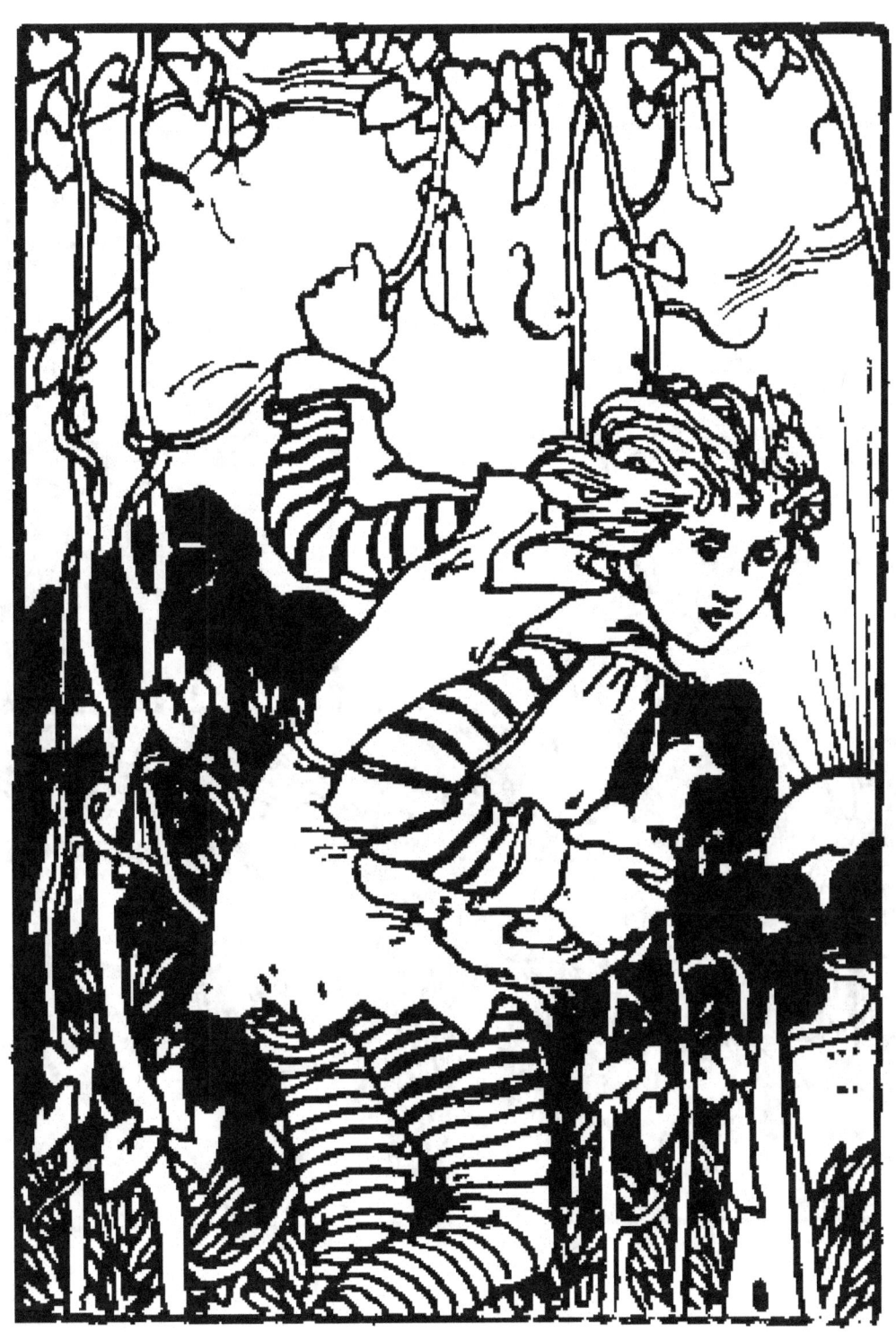

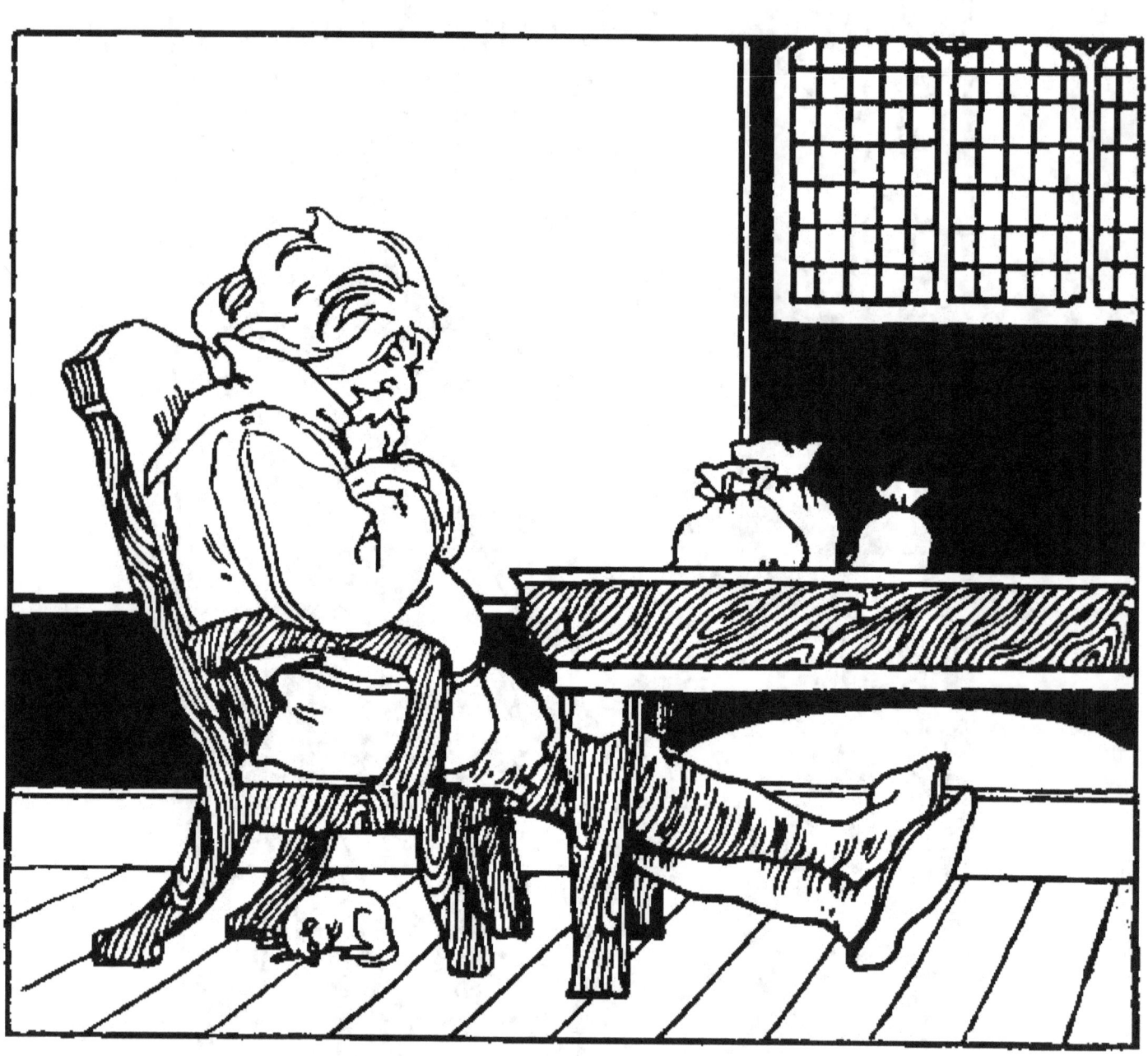

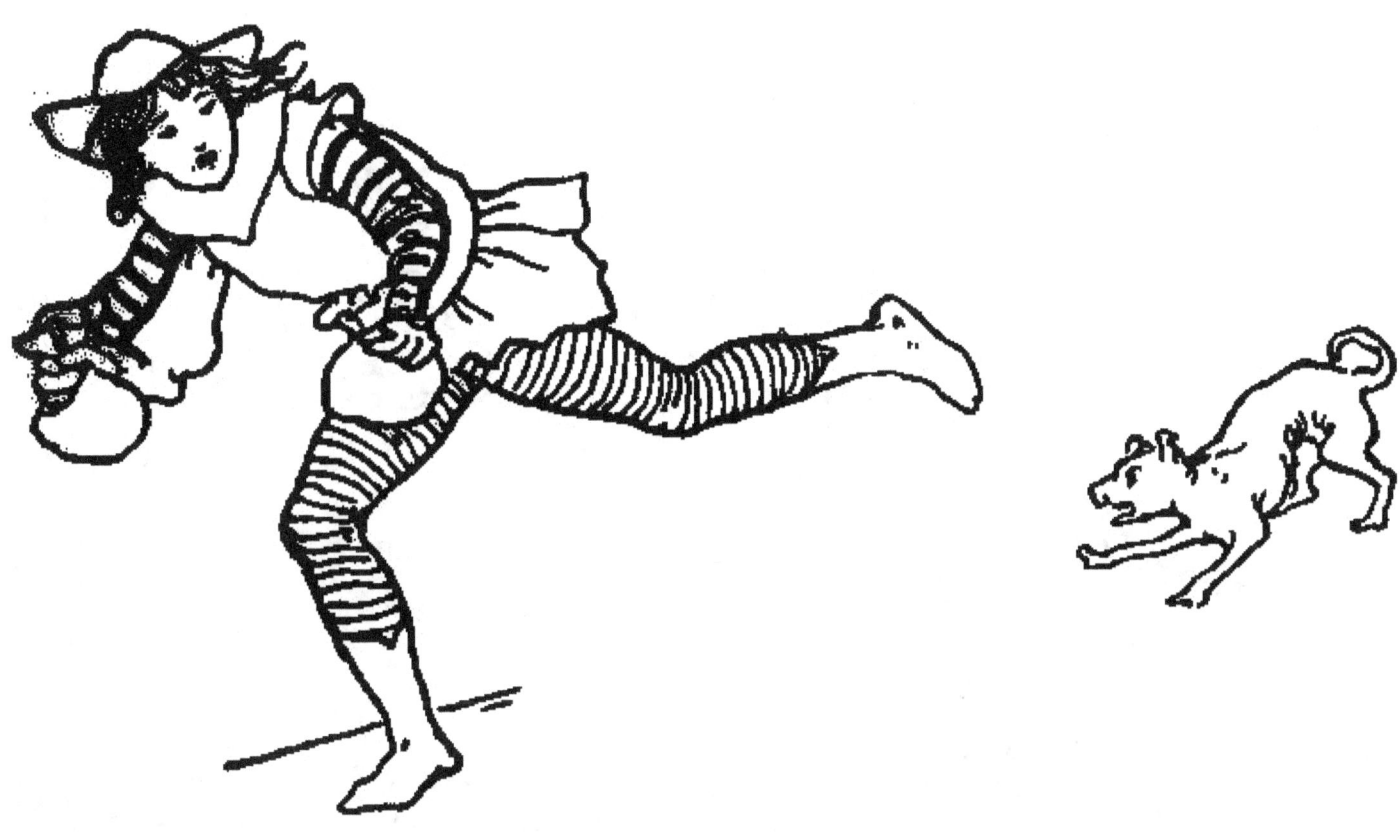

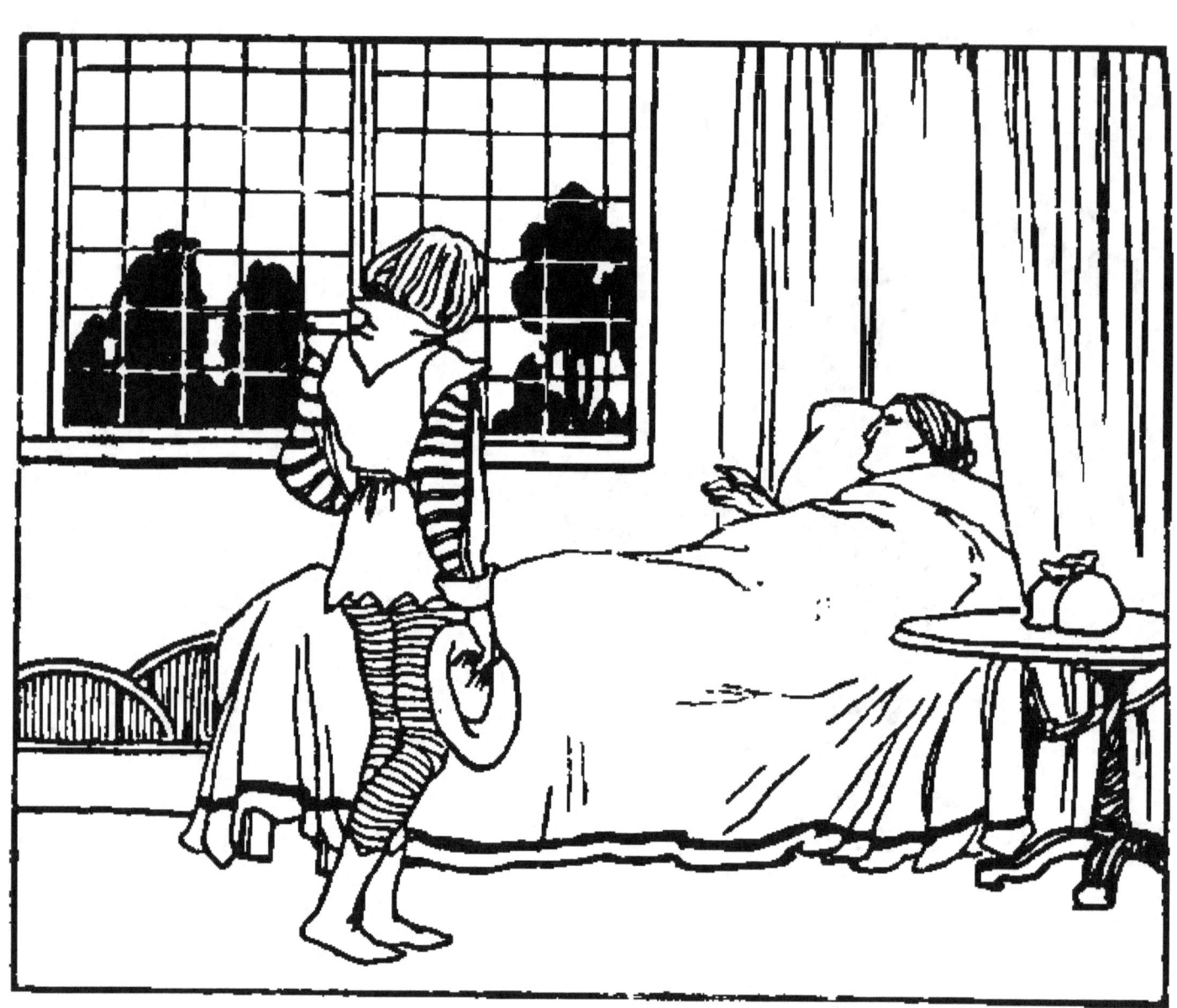

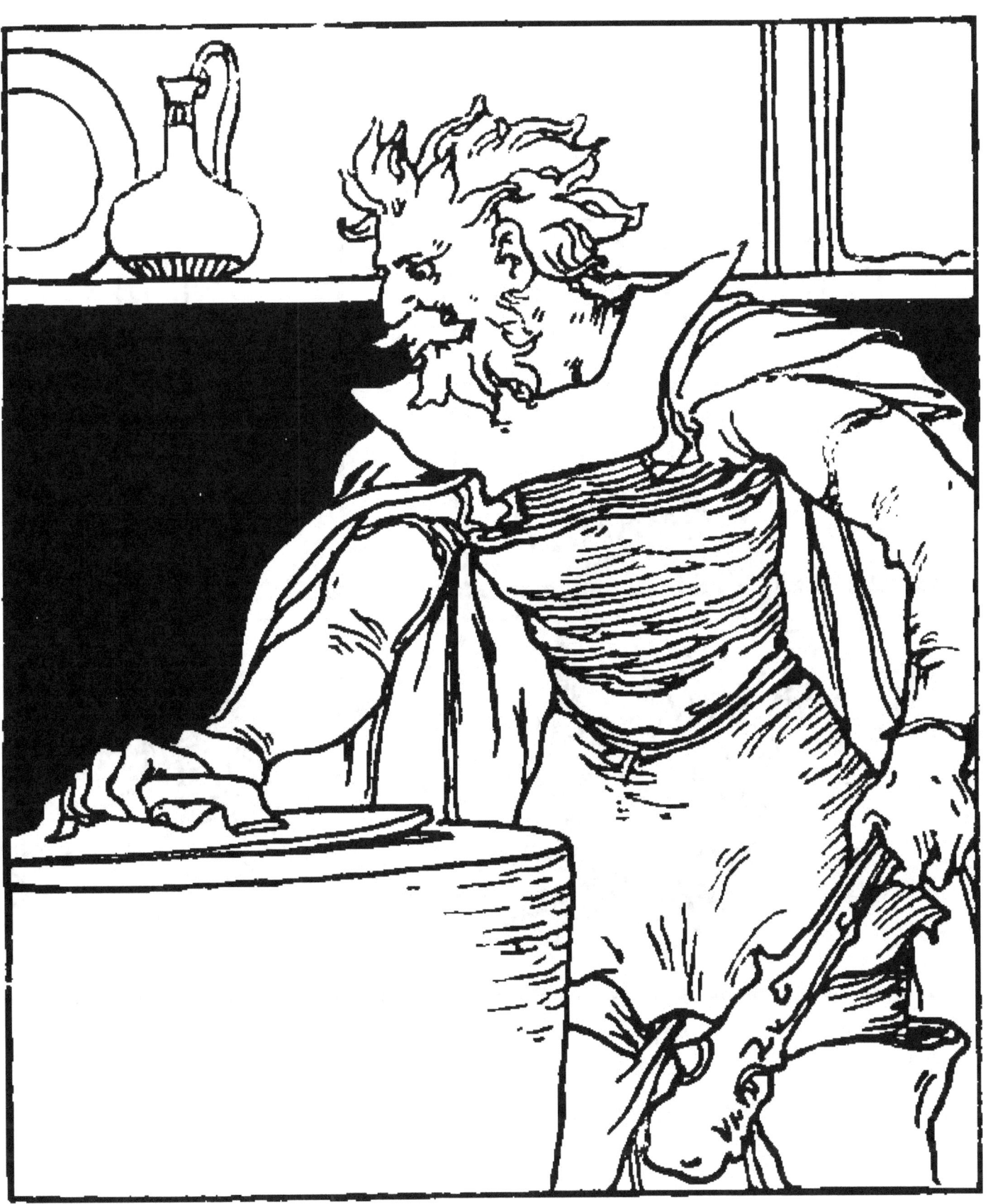

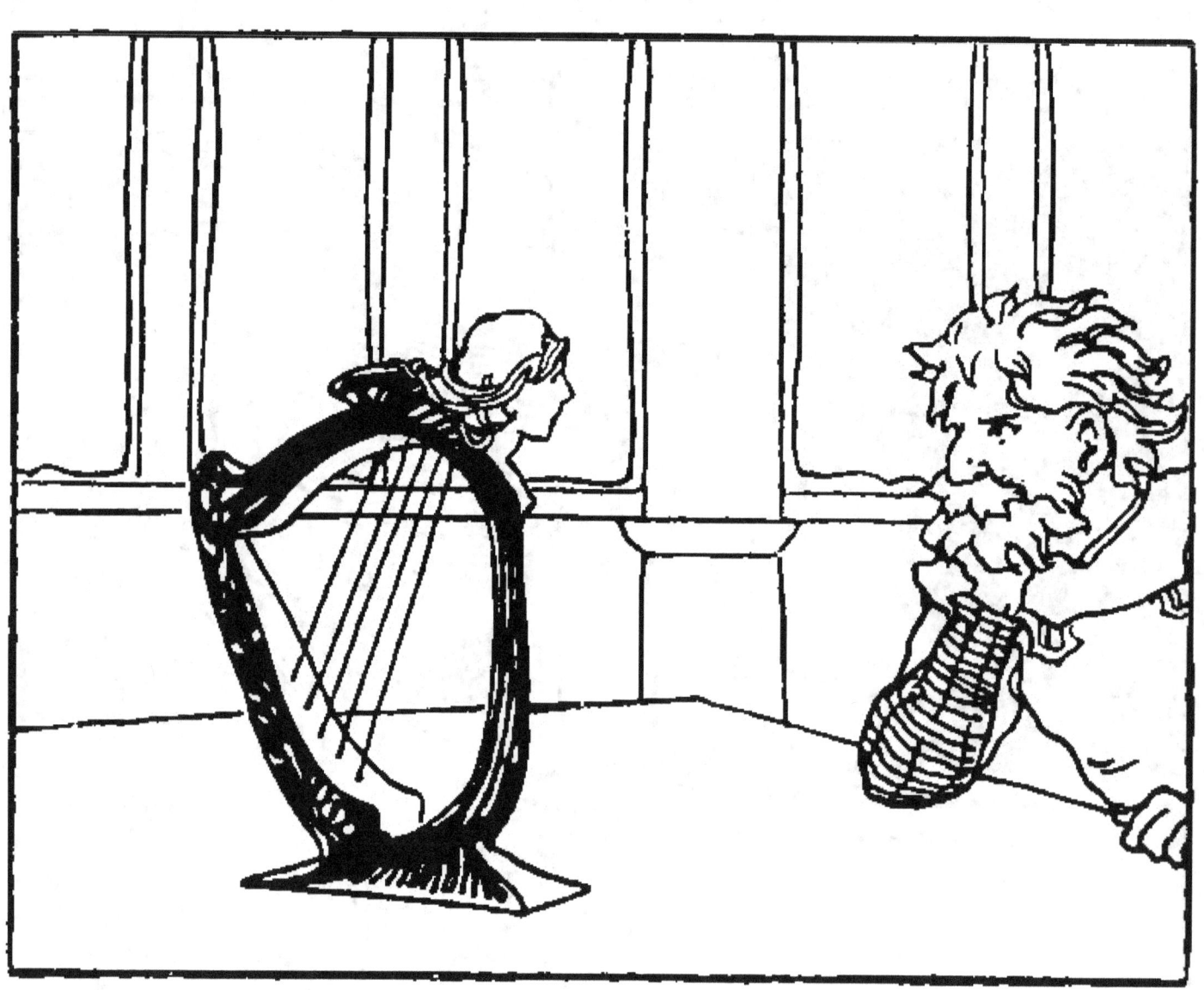

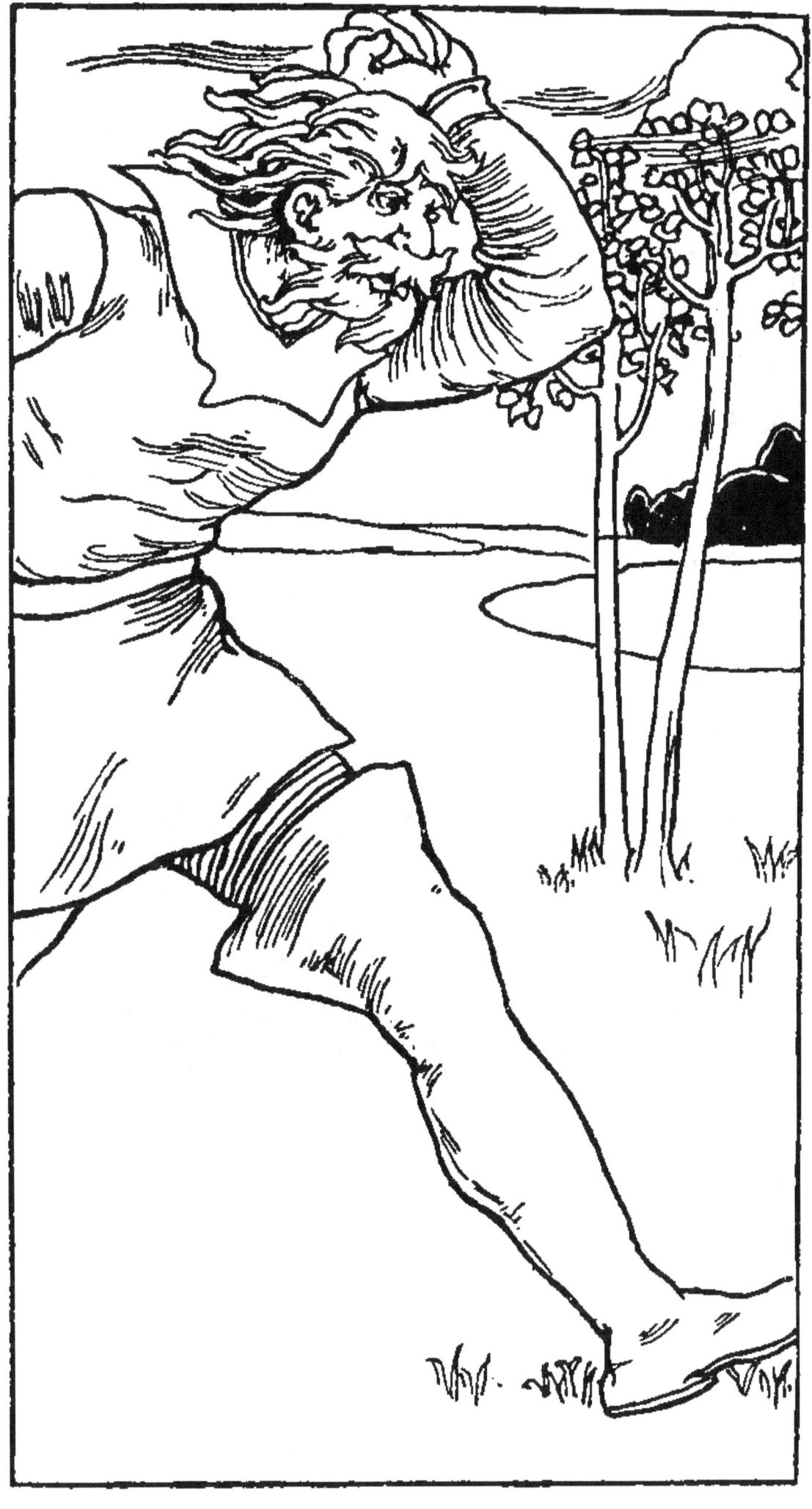

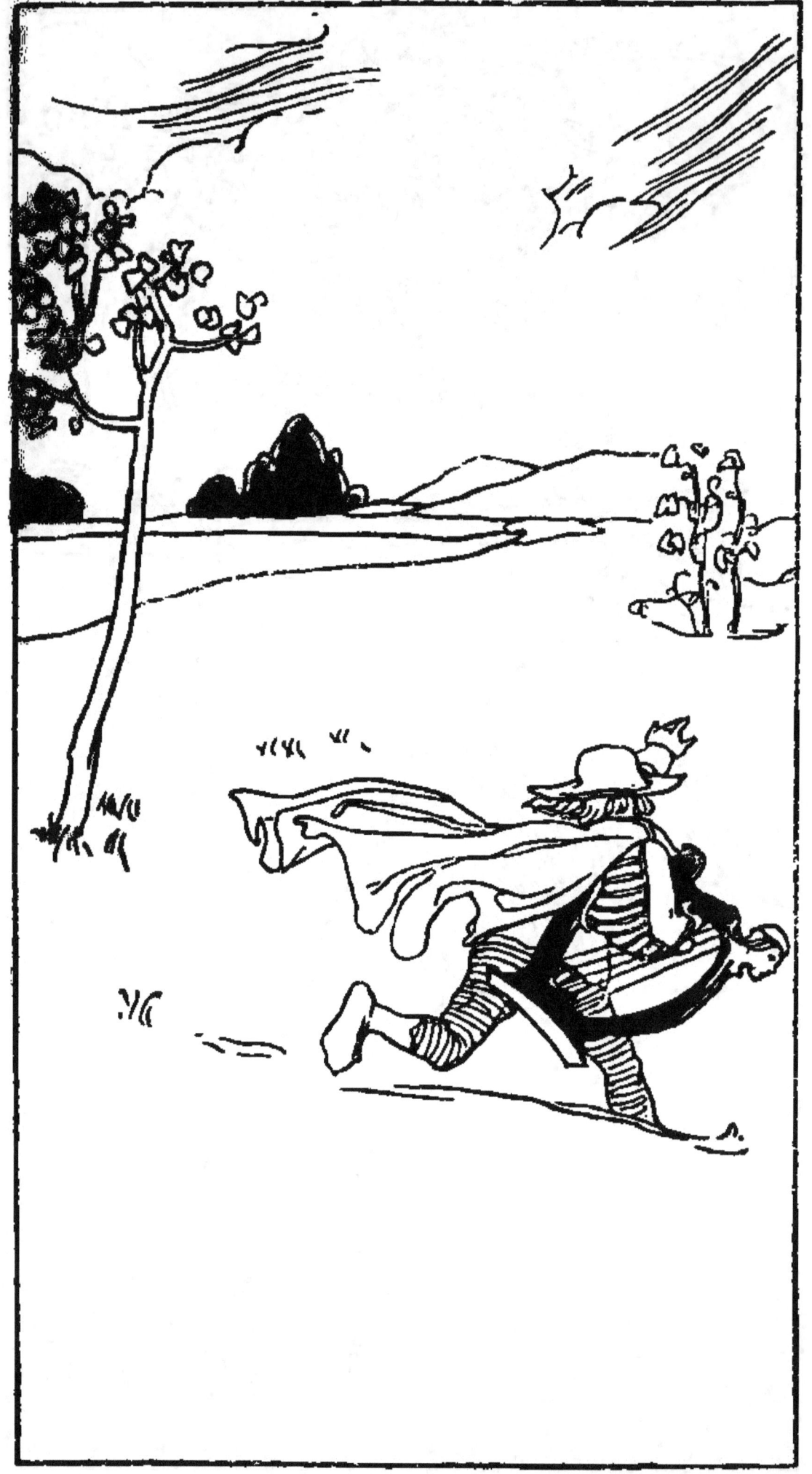

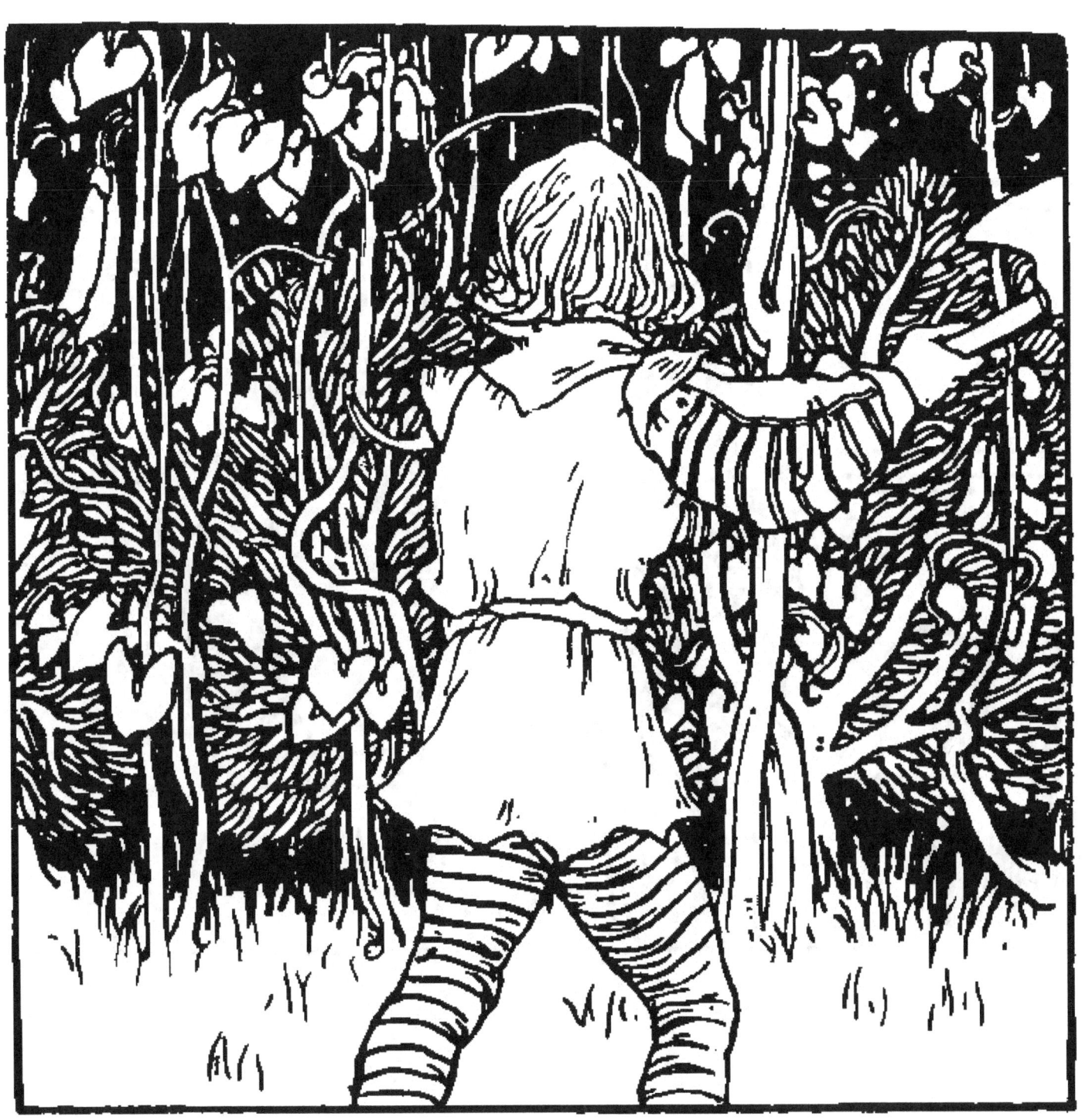

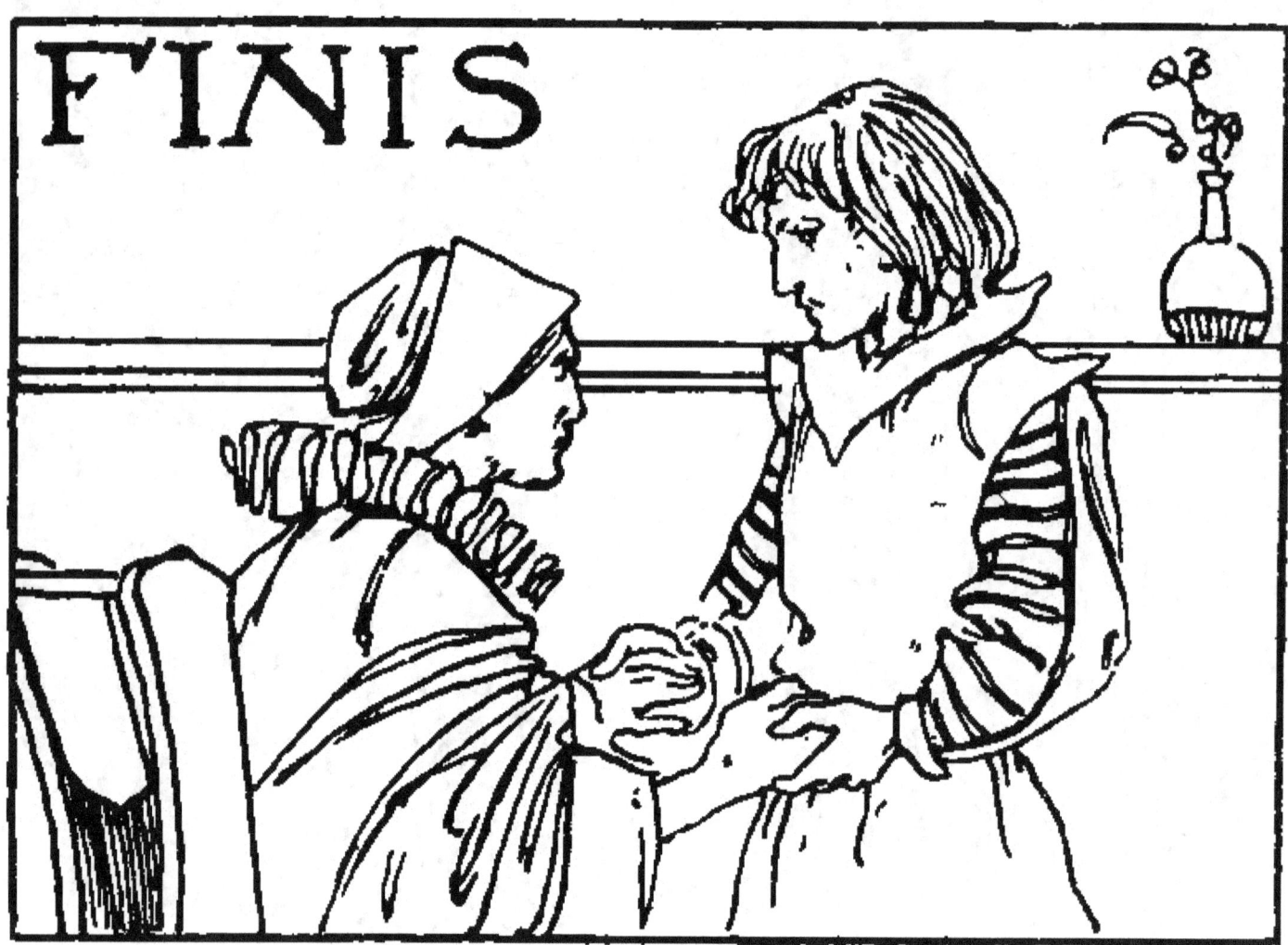

JACK THE GIANT-KILLER AND BEAUTY AND THE BEAST ILLUSTRATED BY R. ANNING BELL

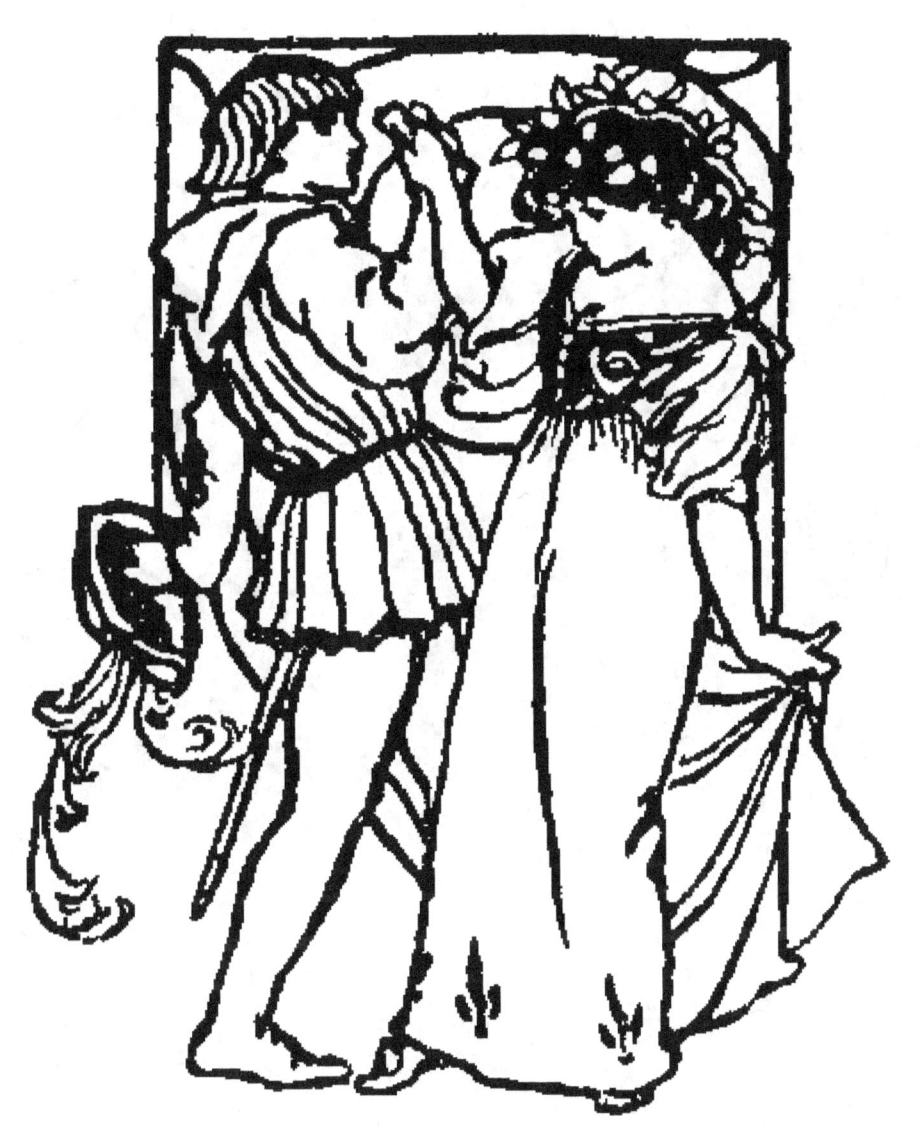

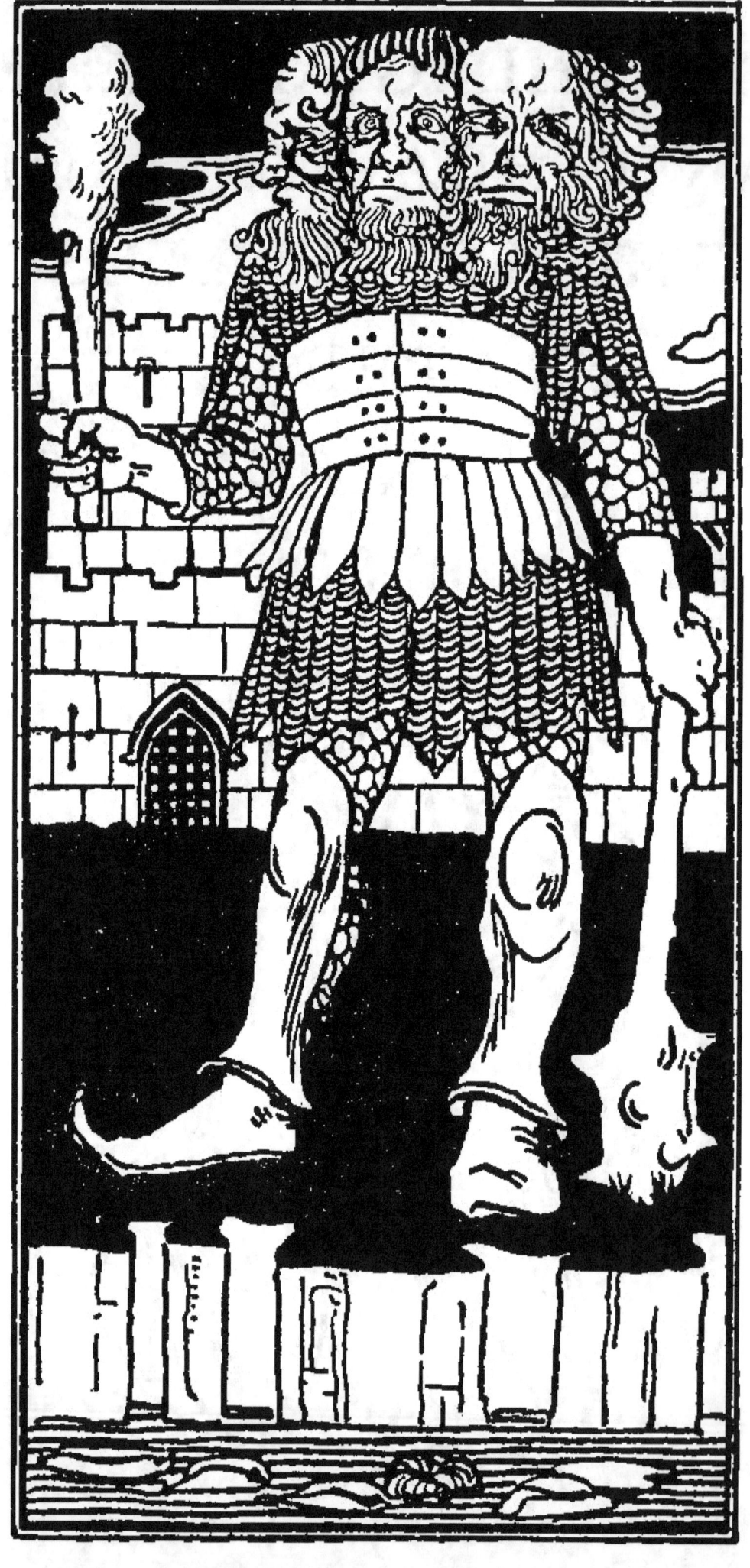

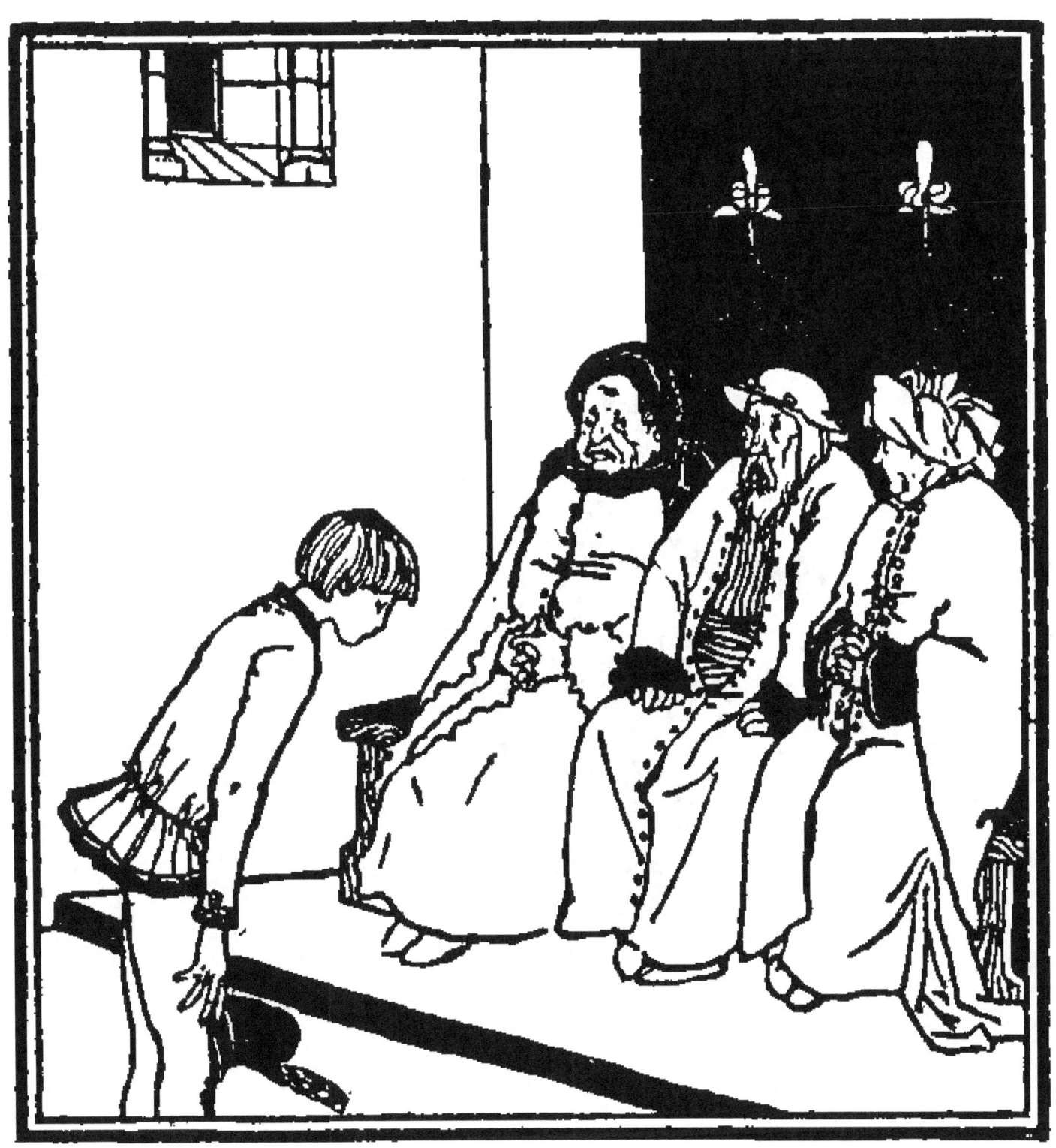

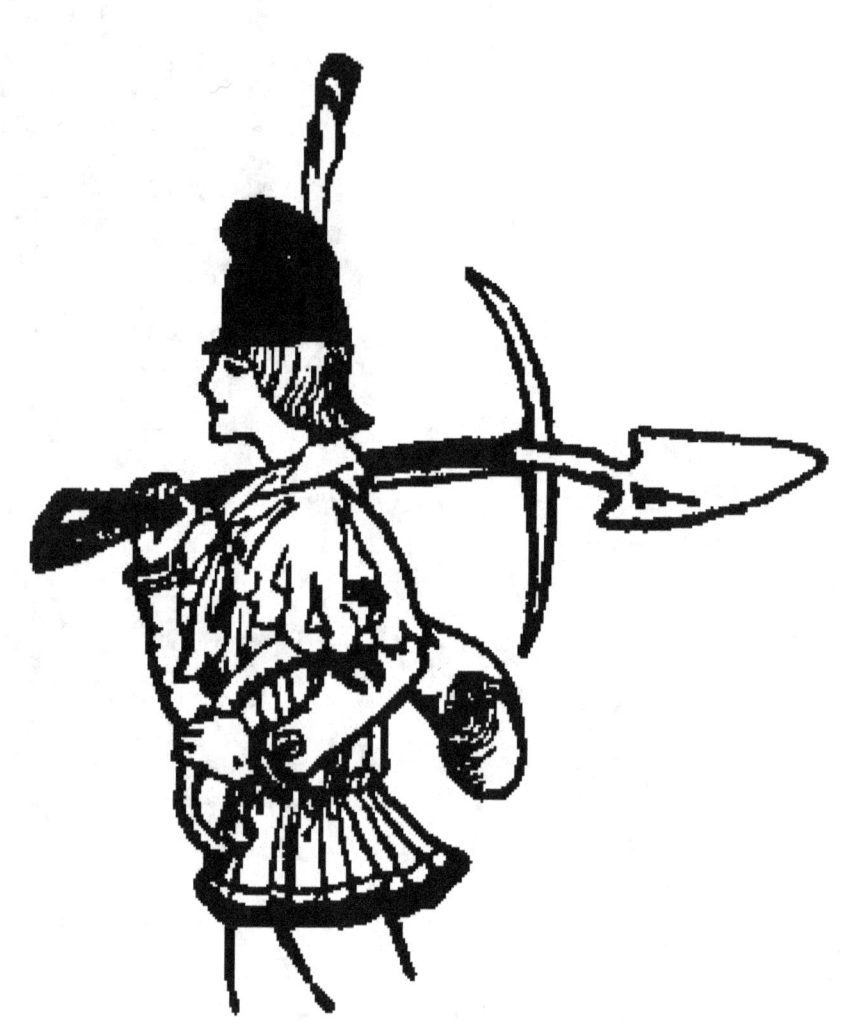

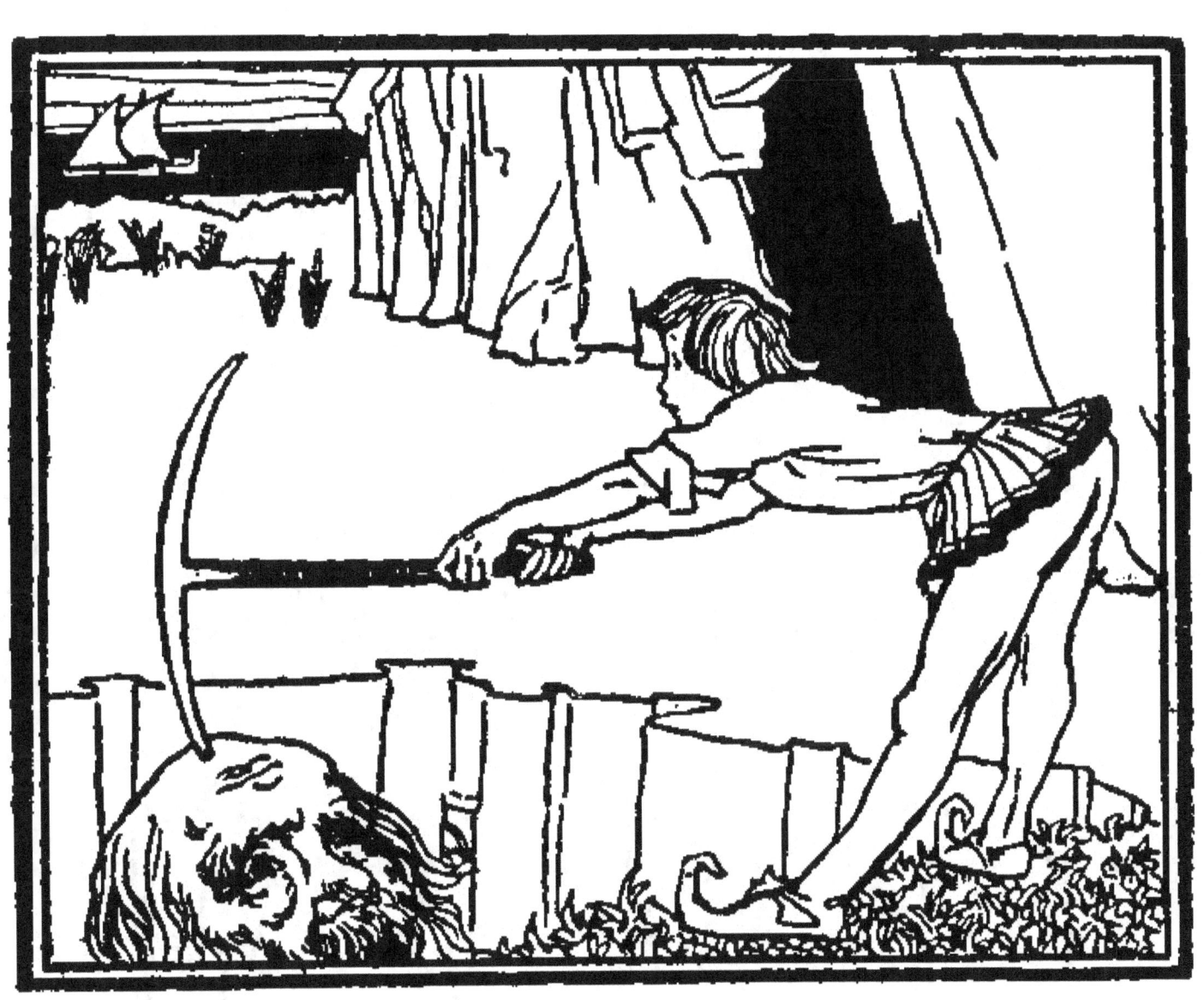

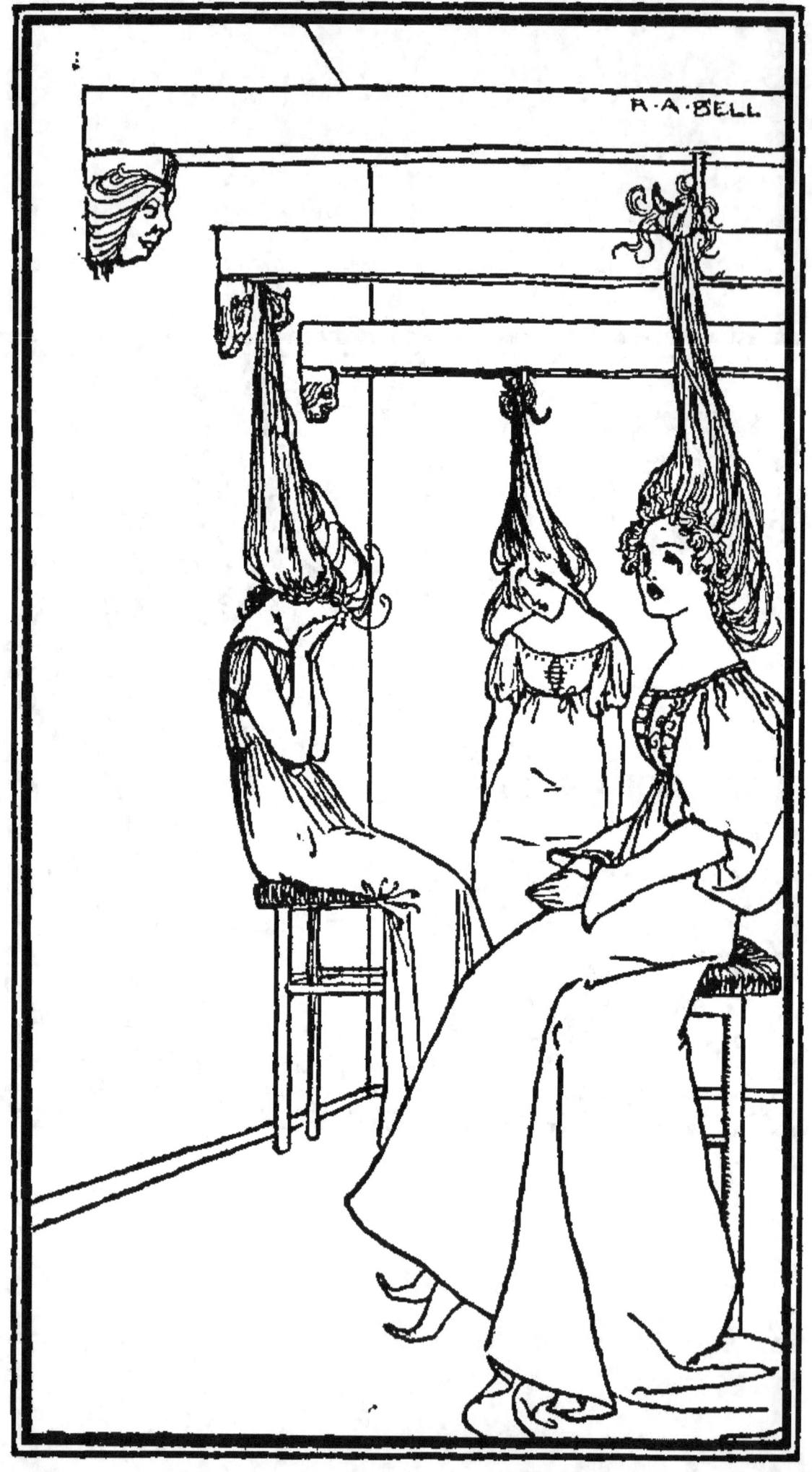

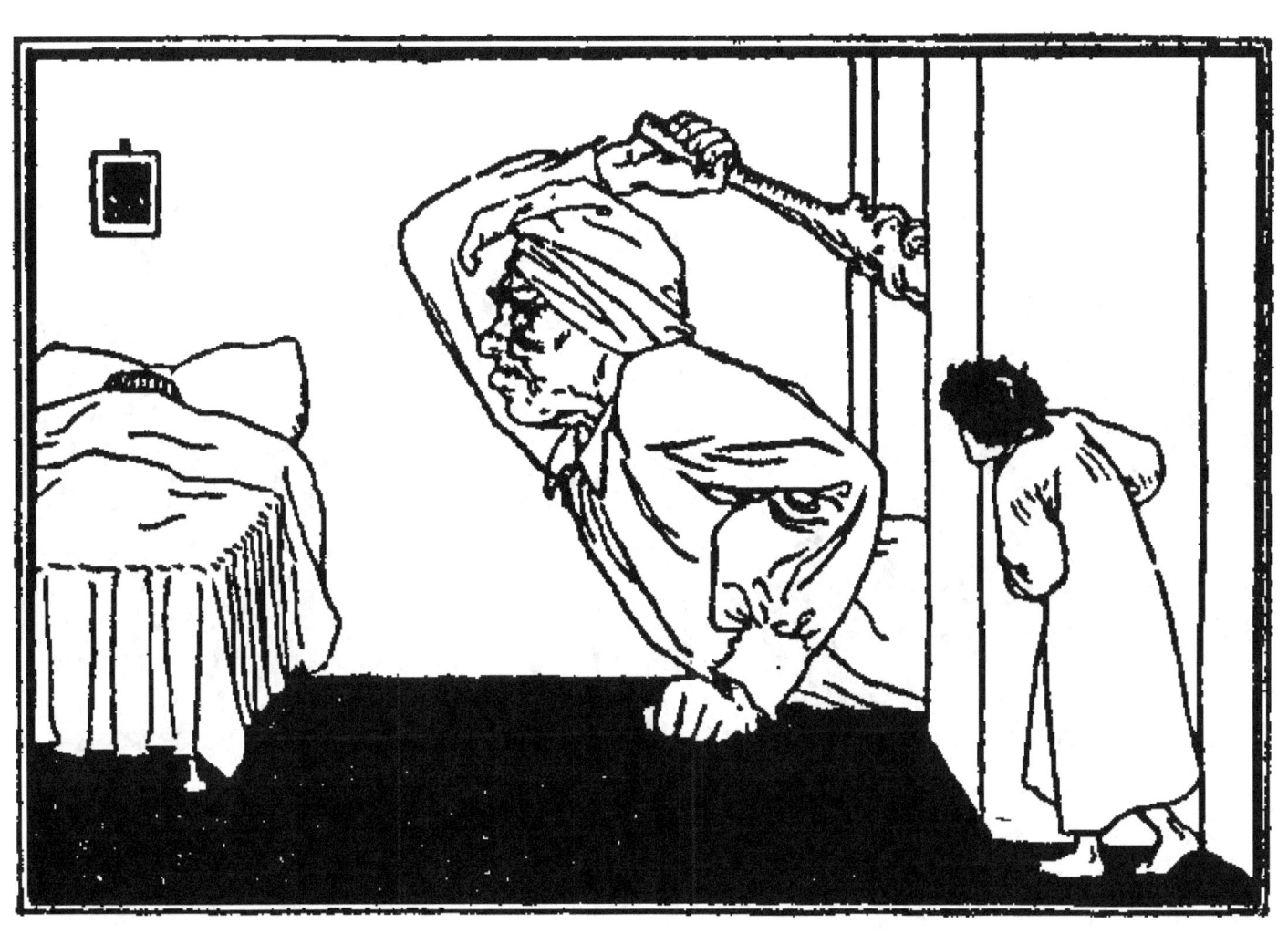

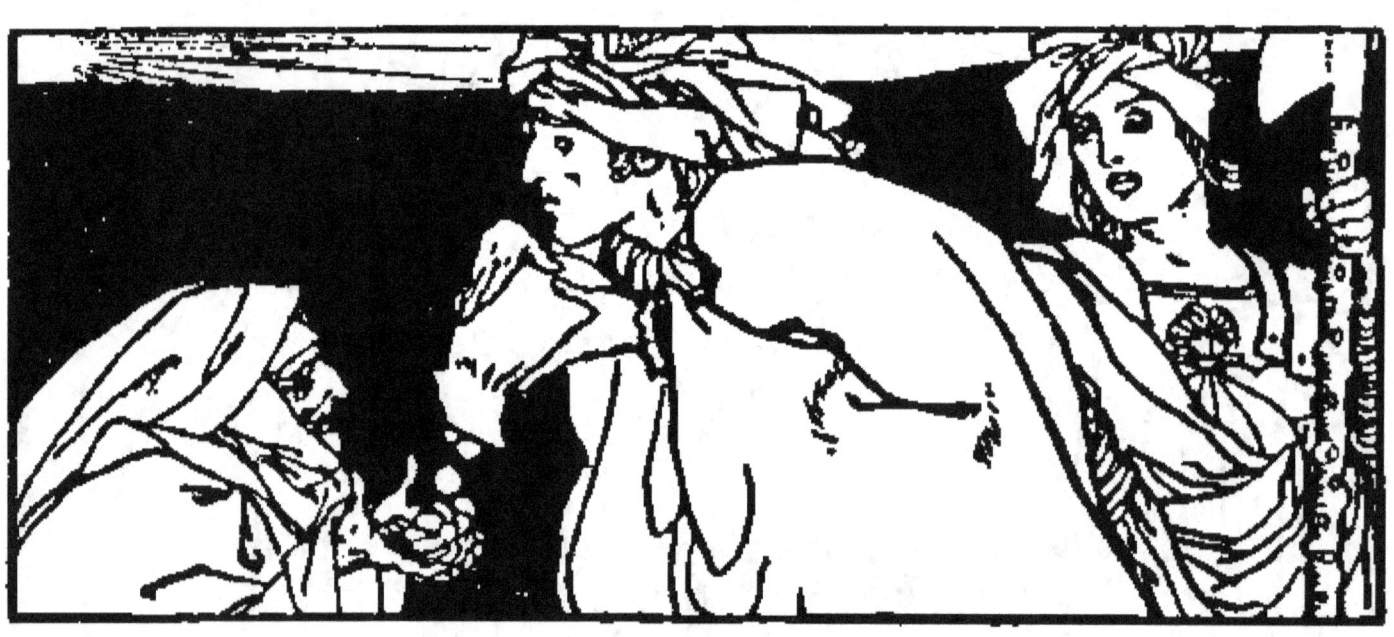

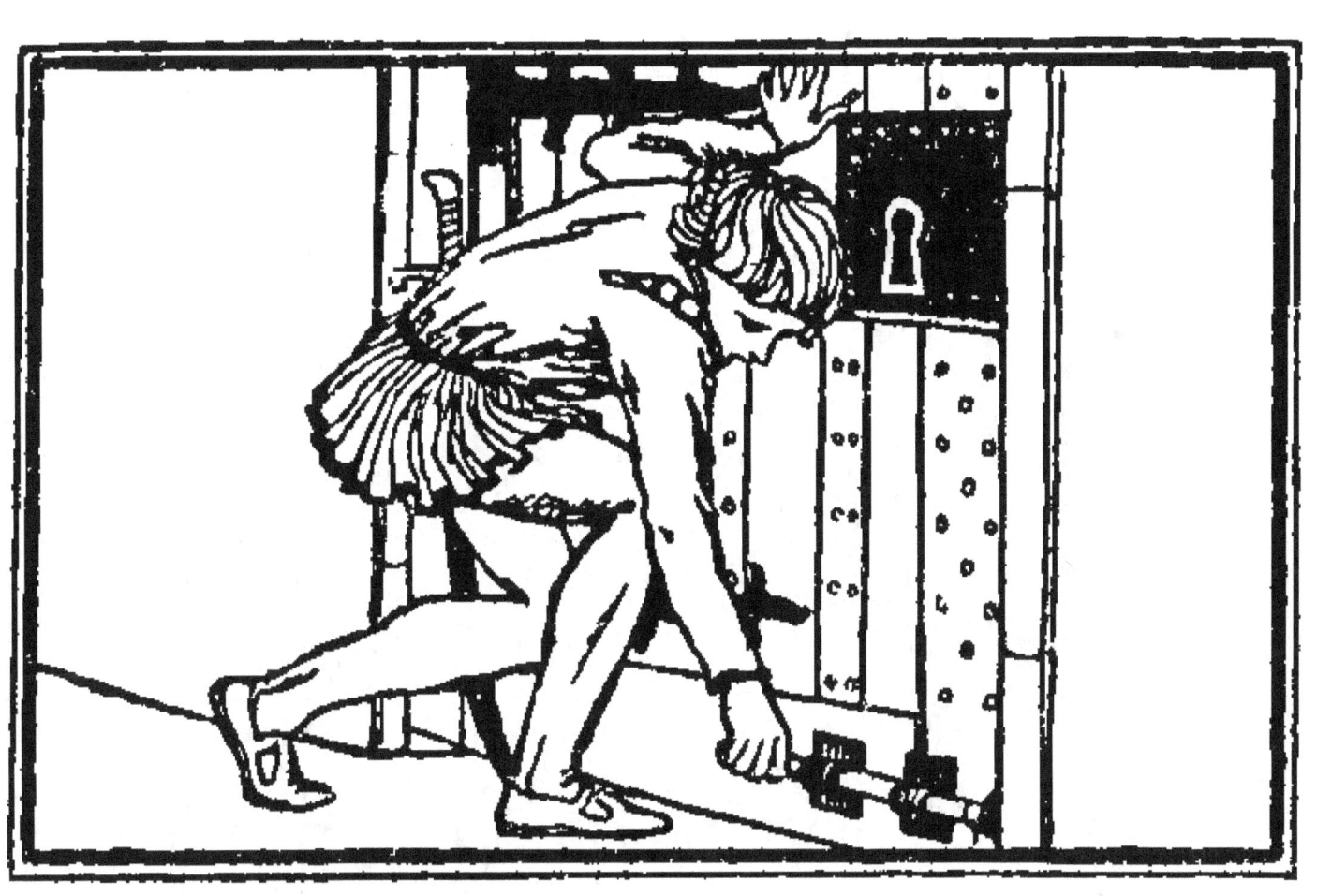

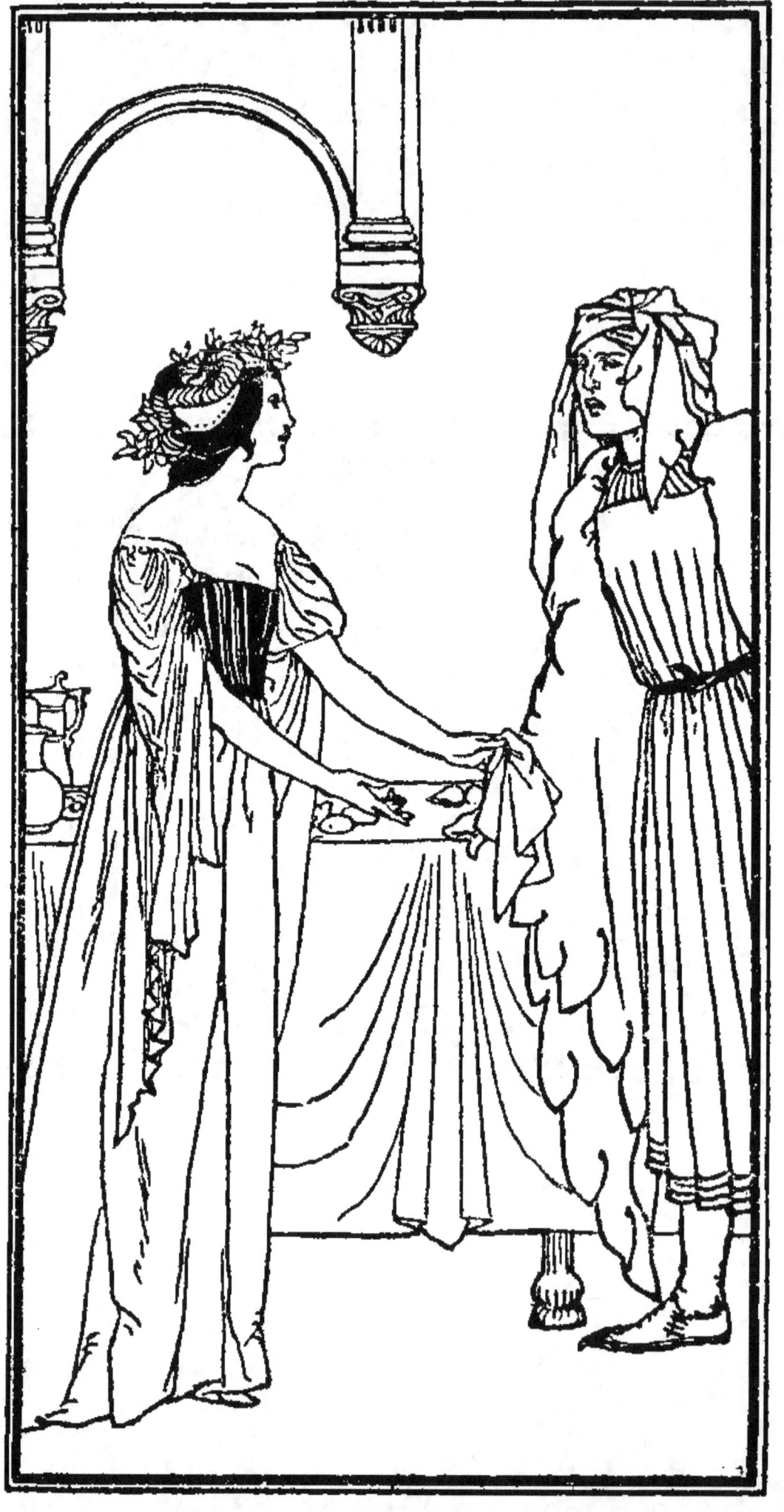

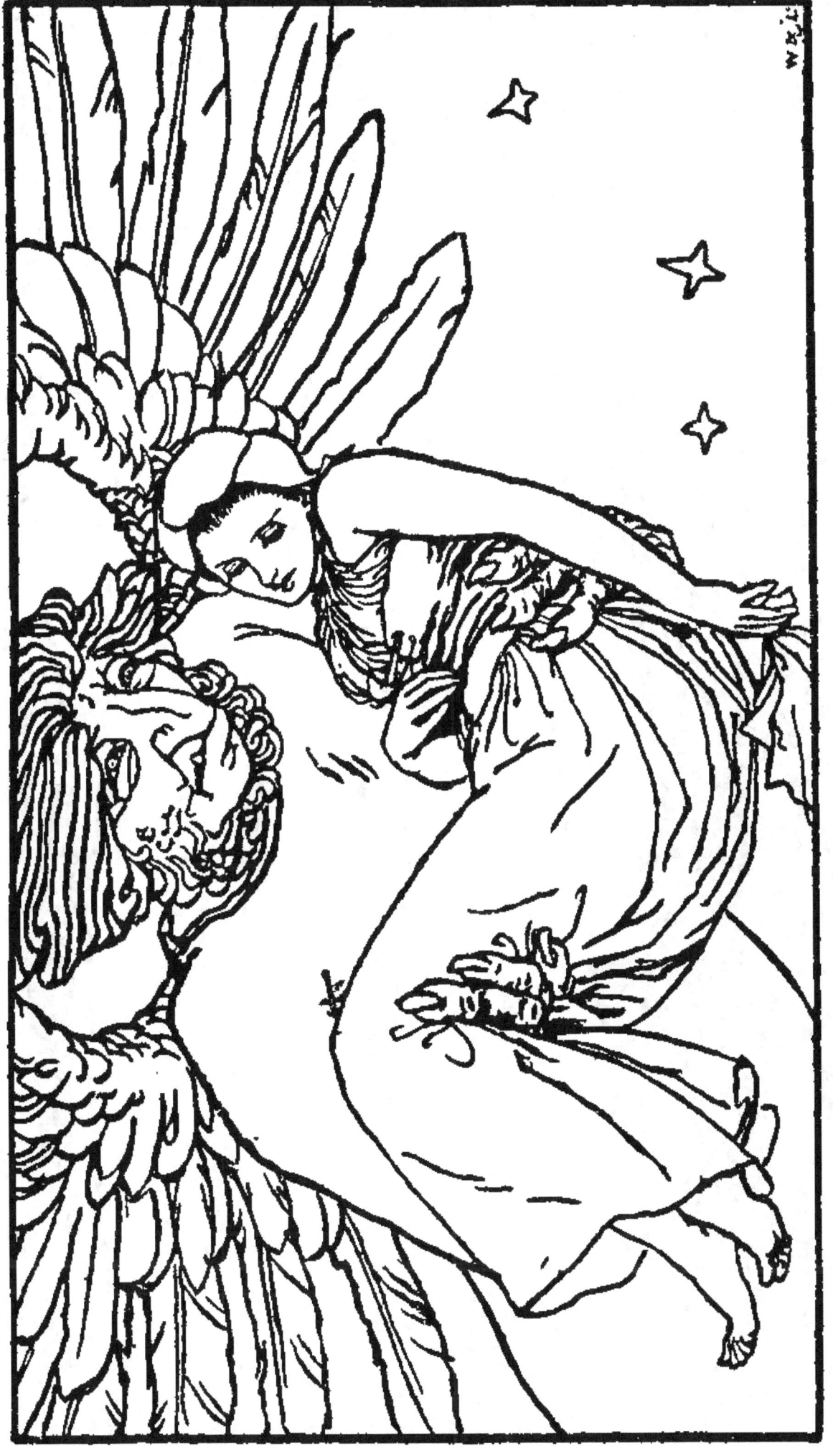

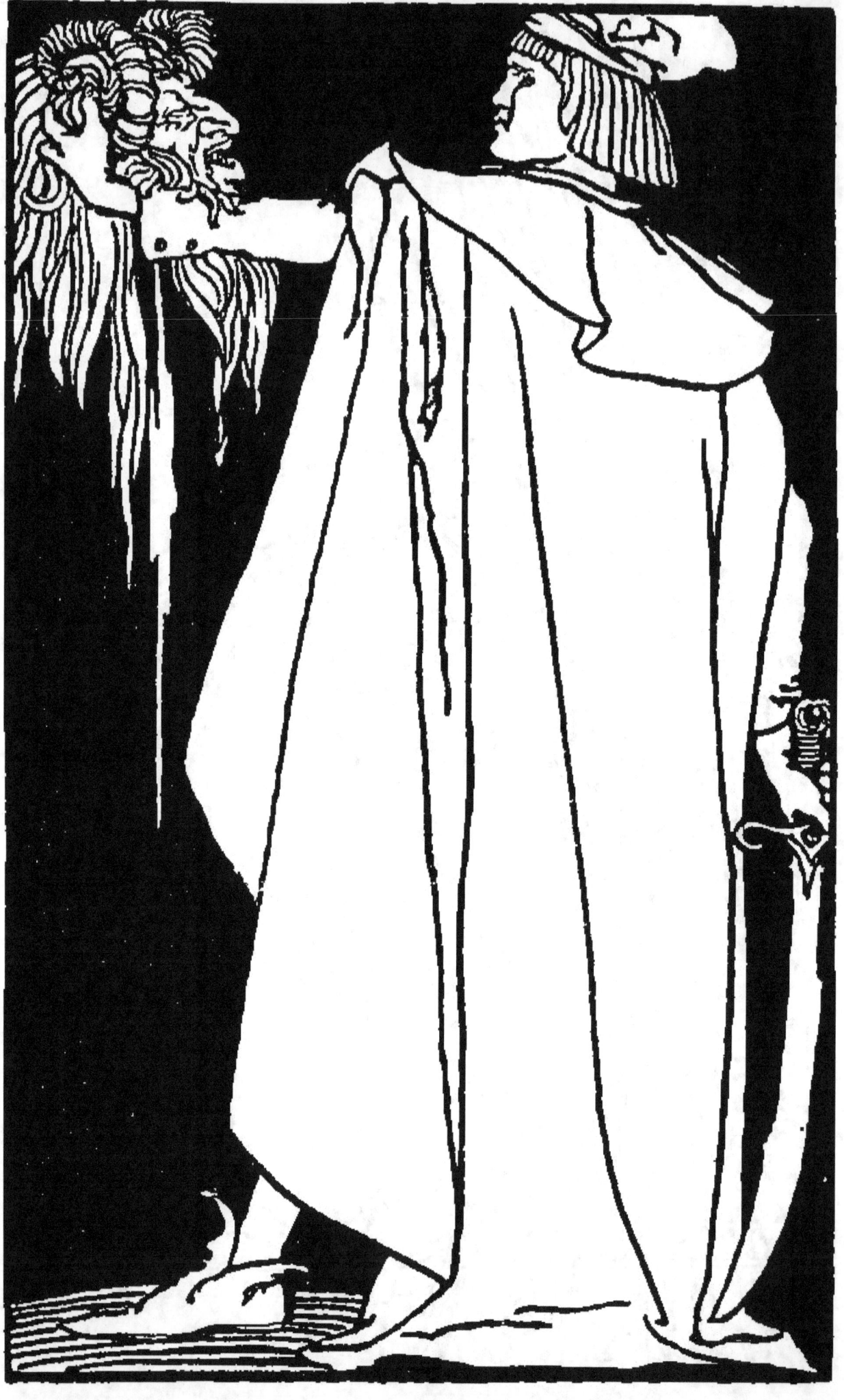

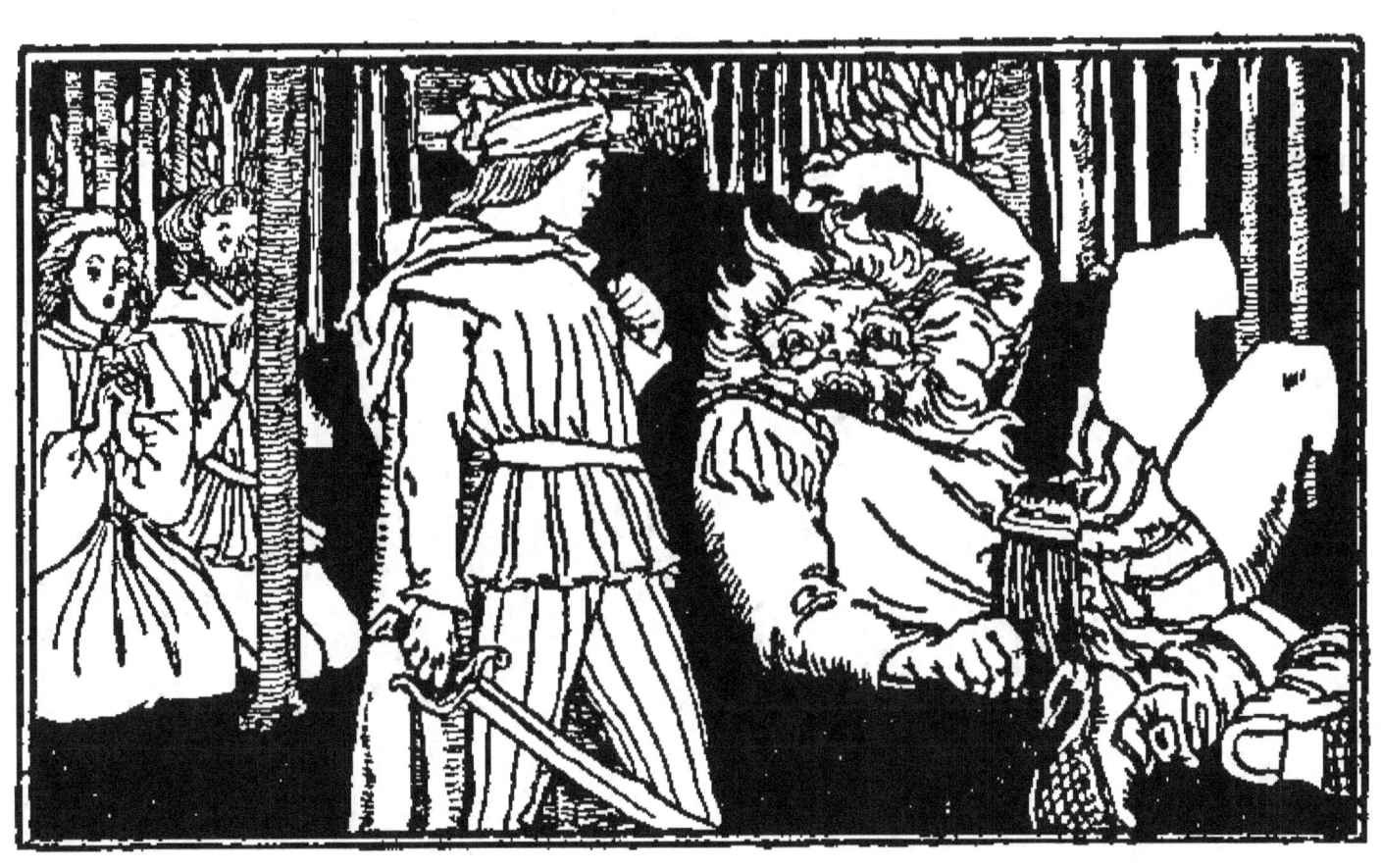

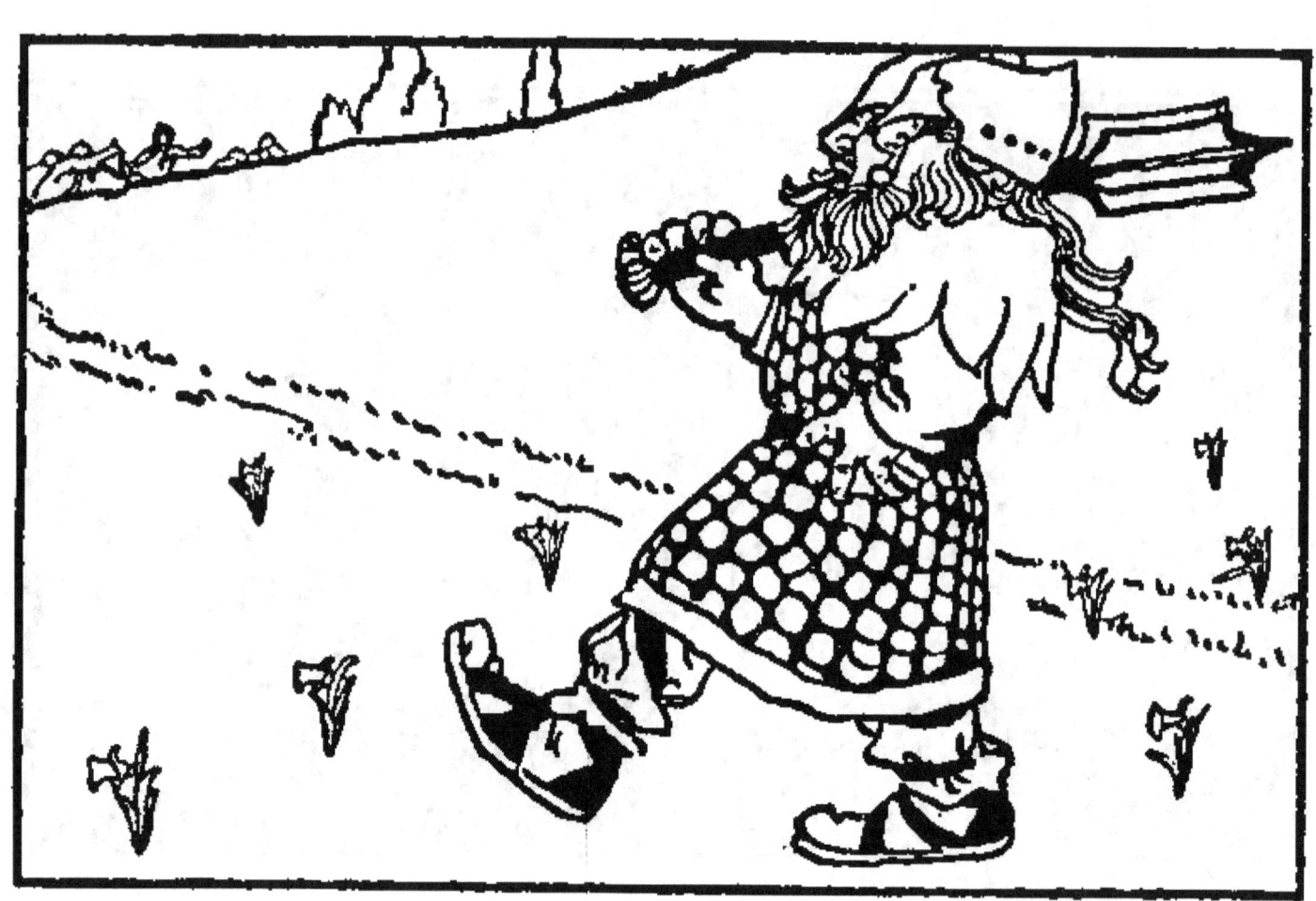

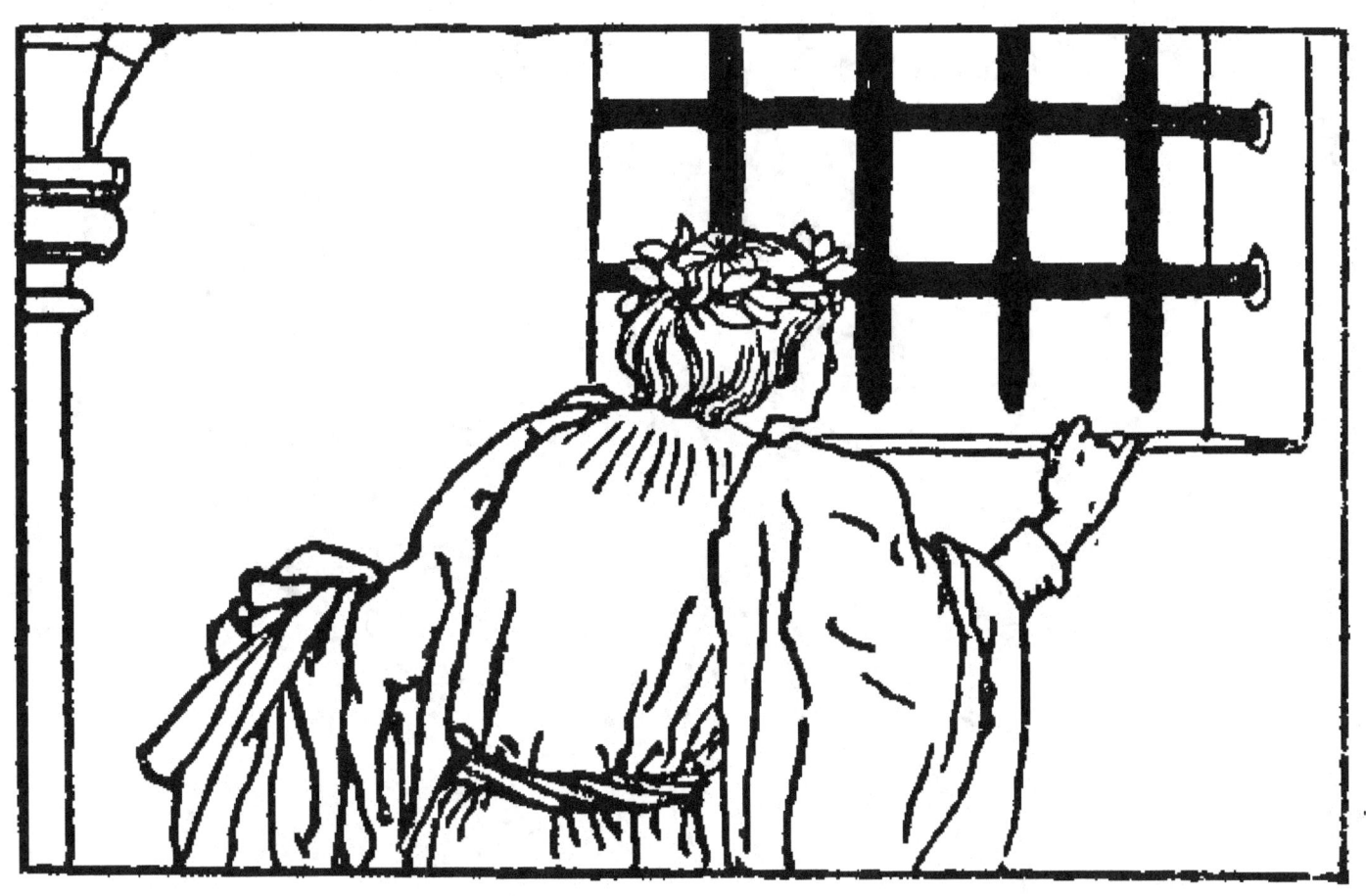

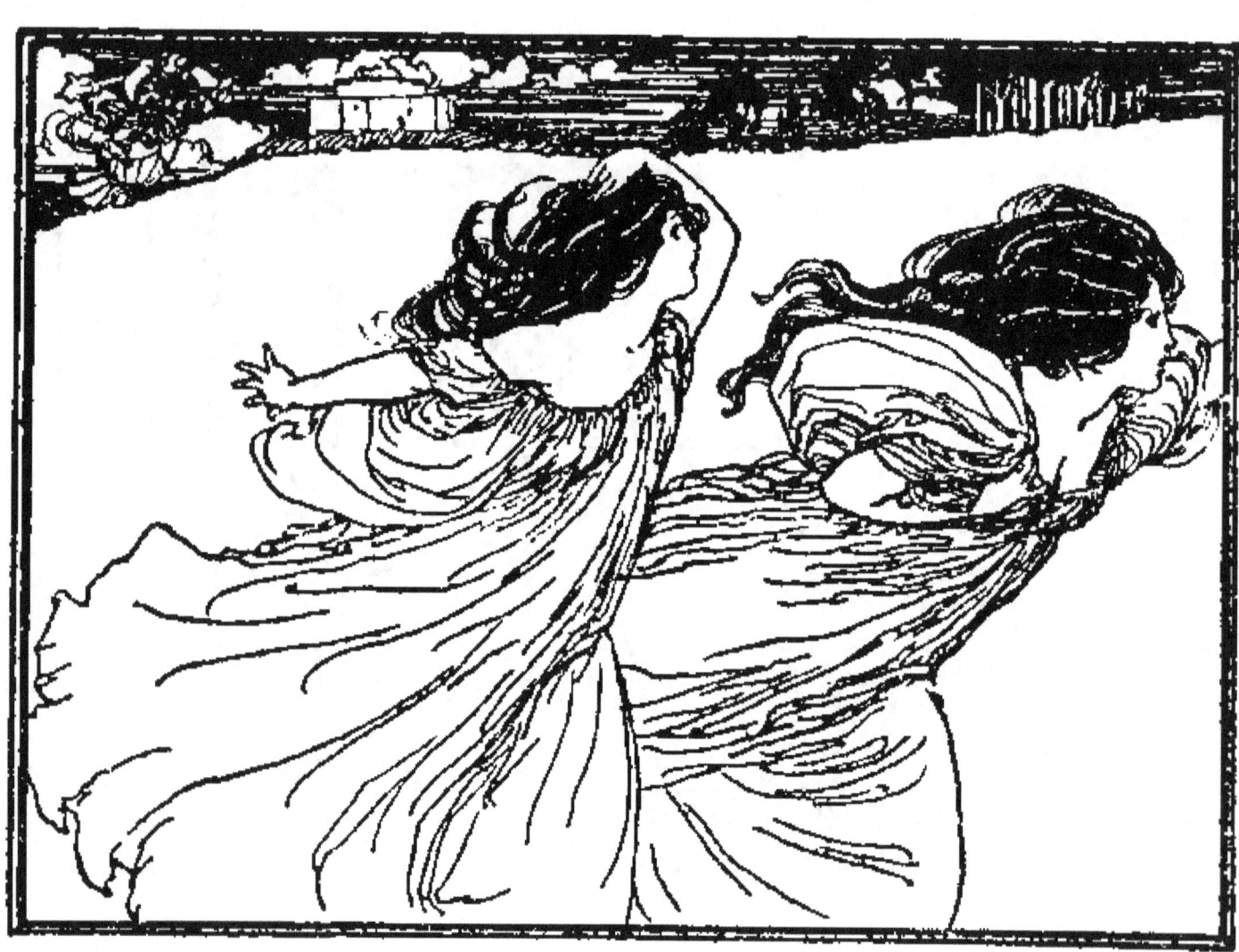

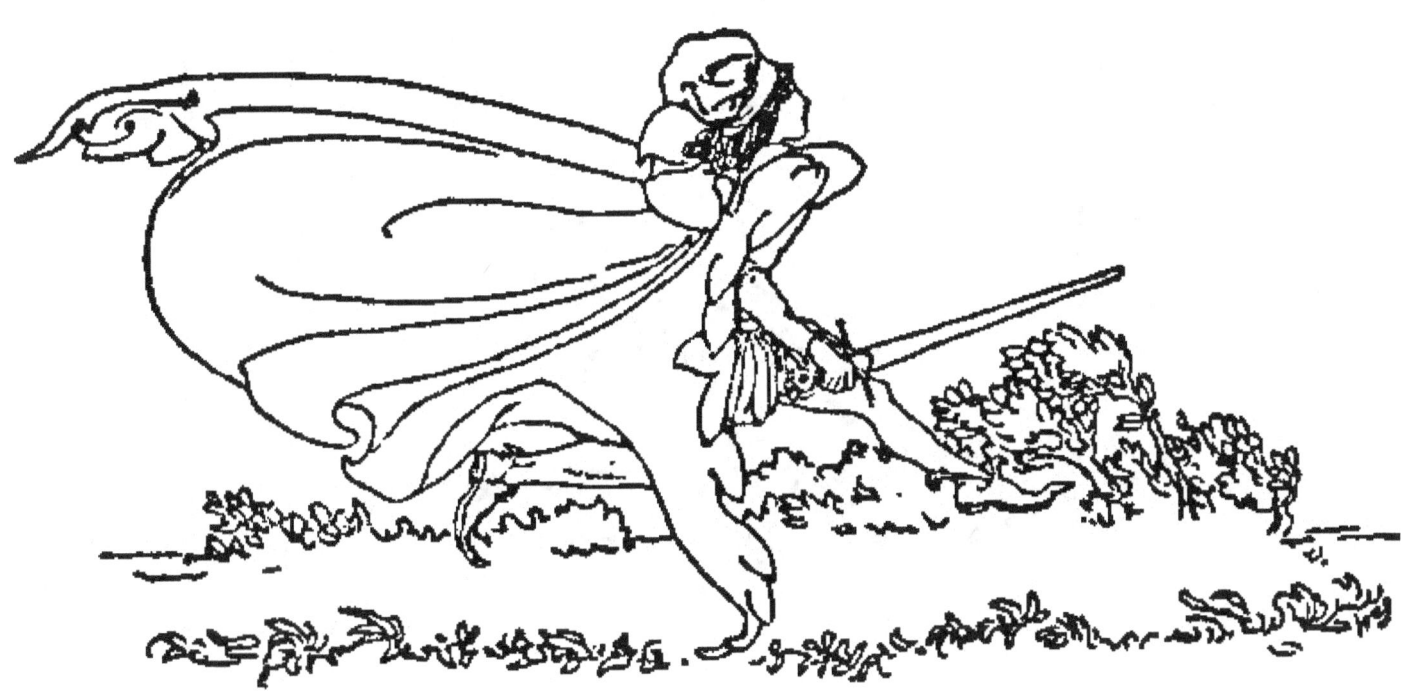

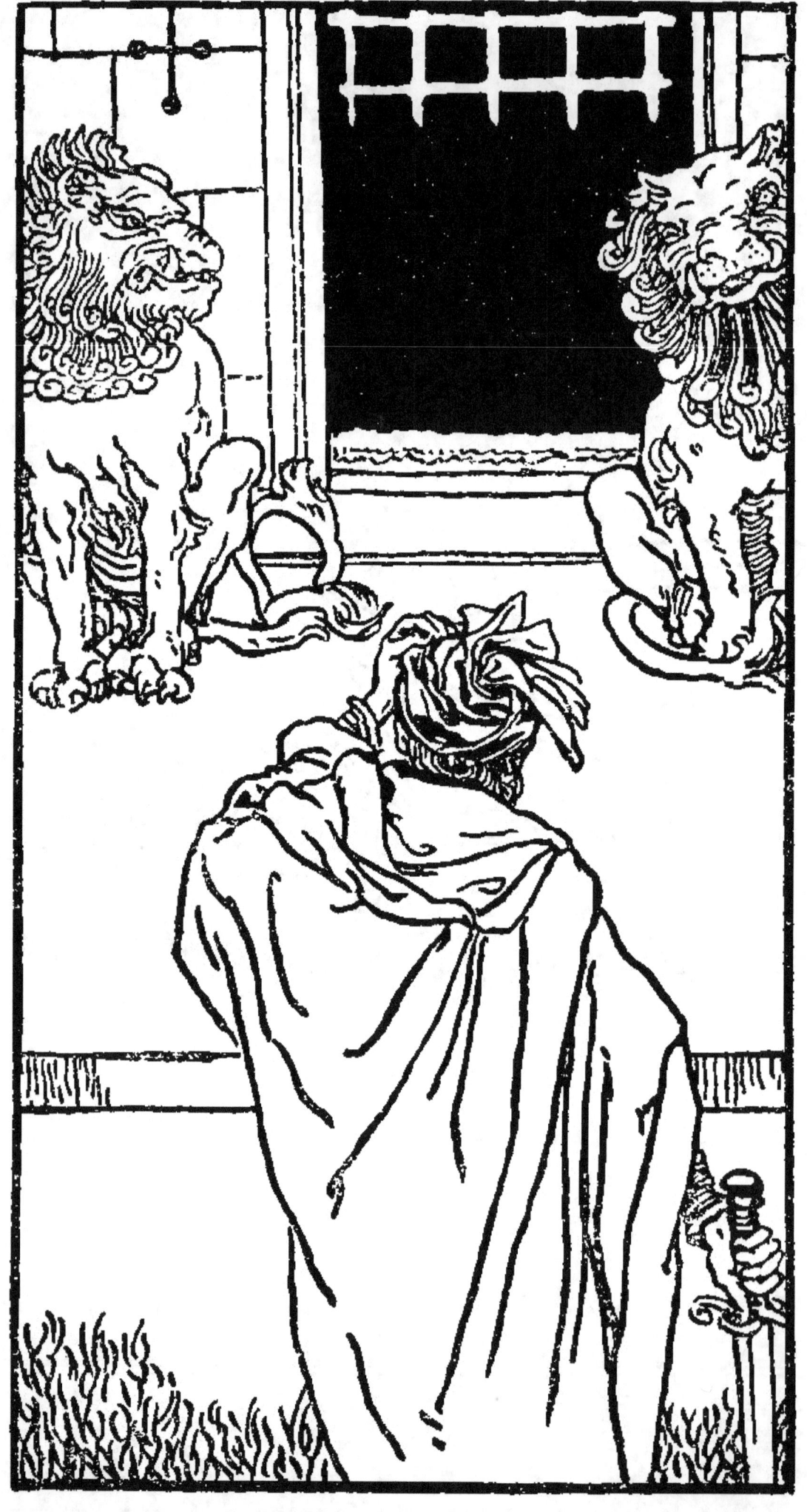

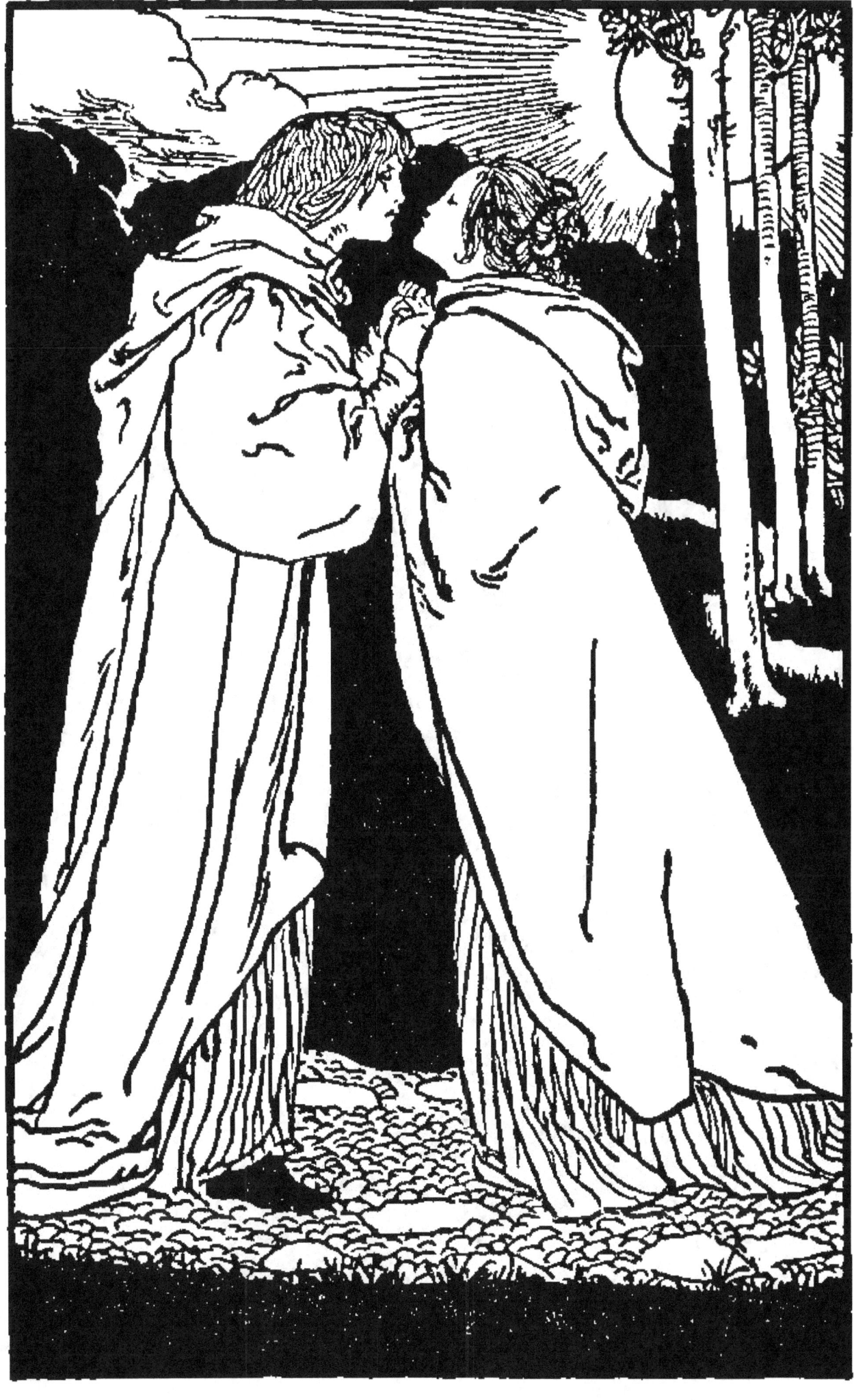

The History of Beauty and the Beast

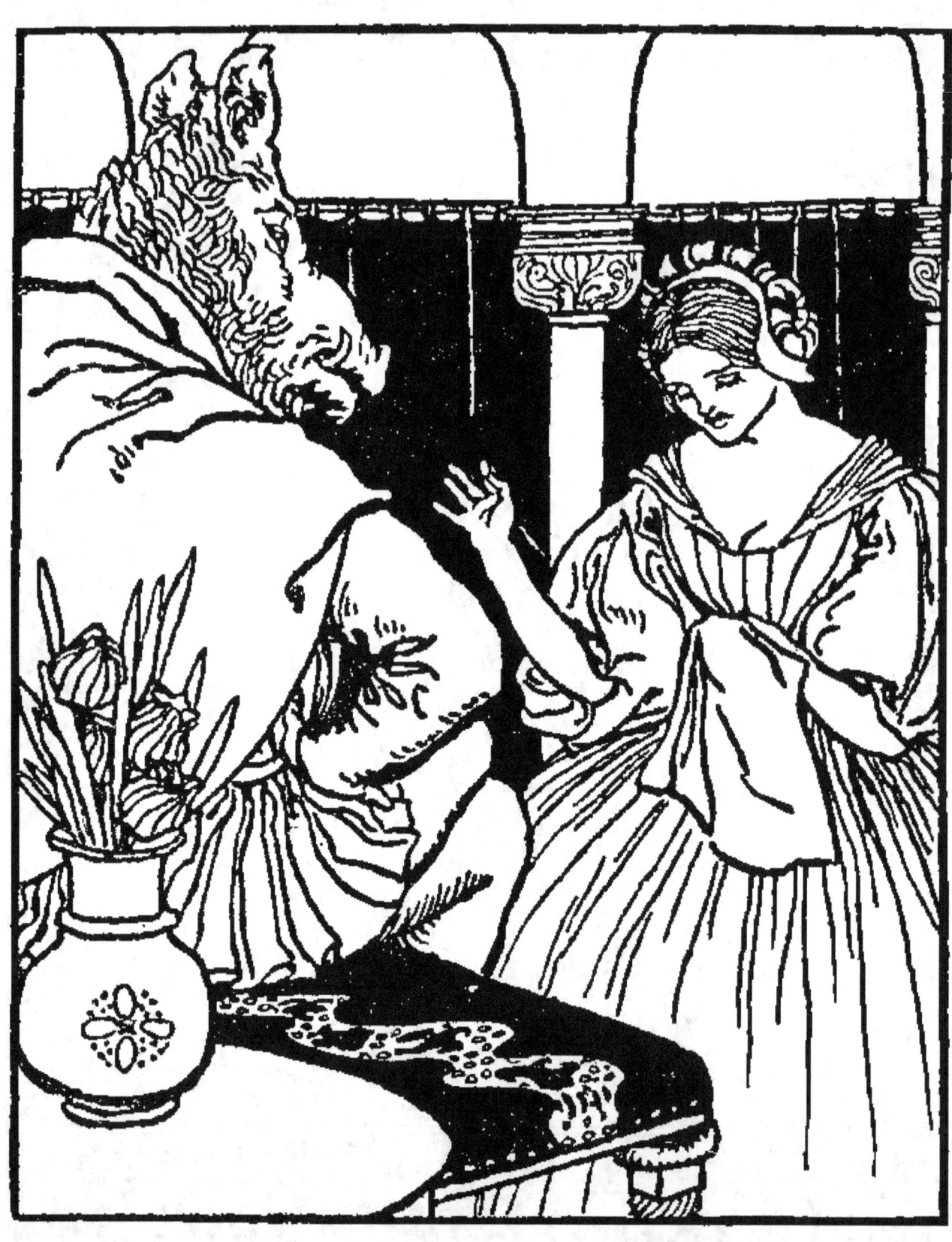

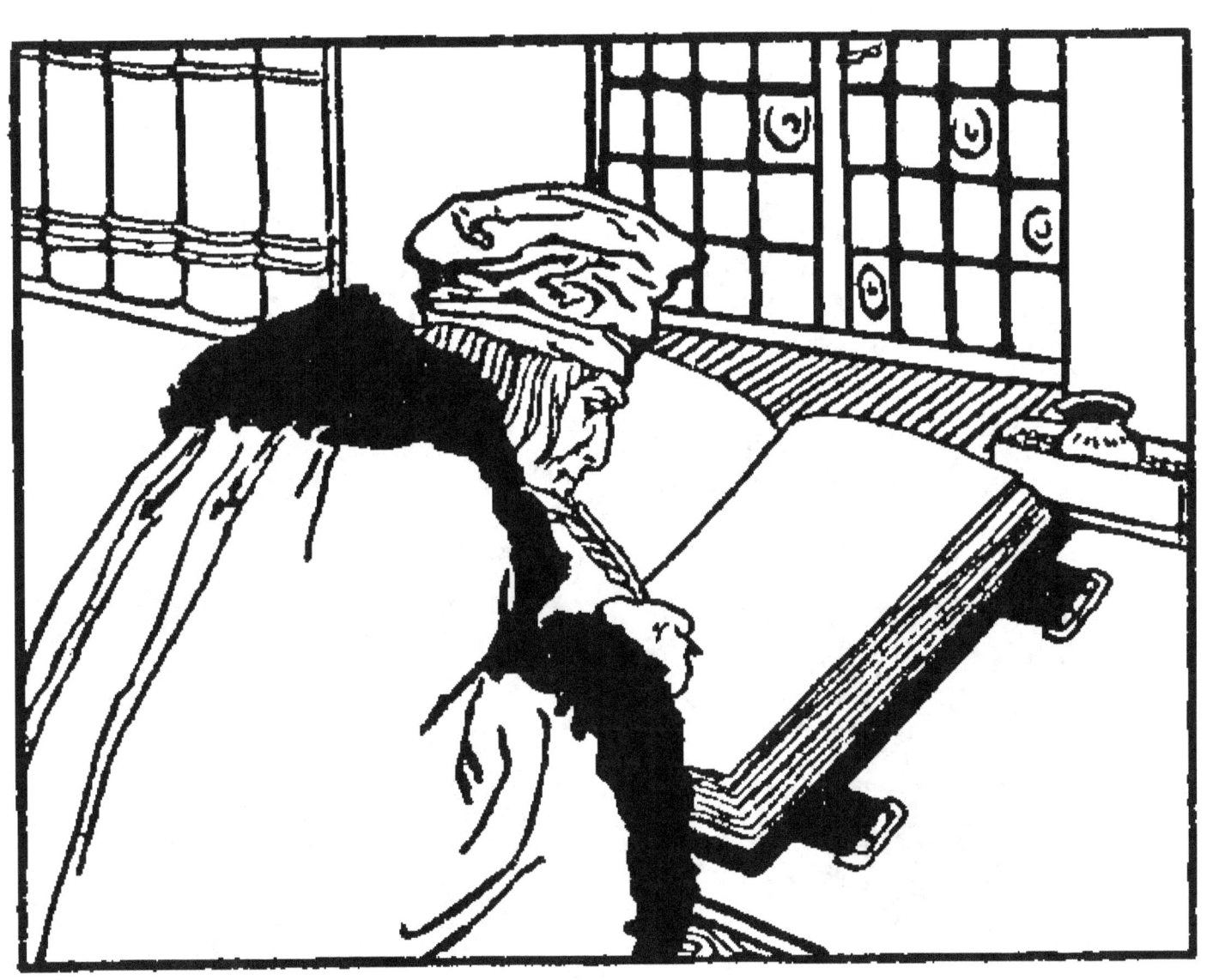

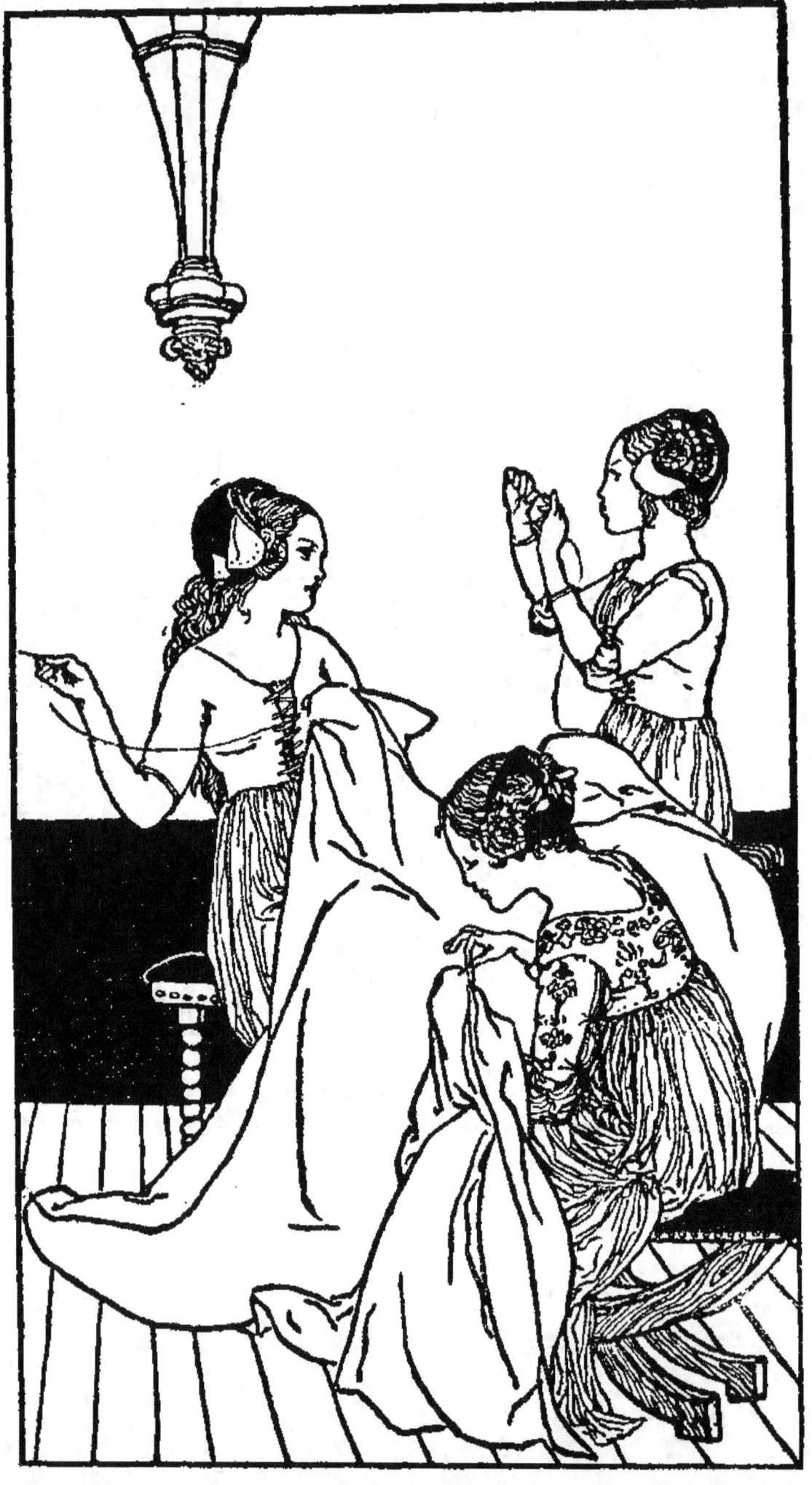

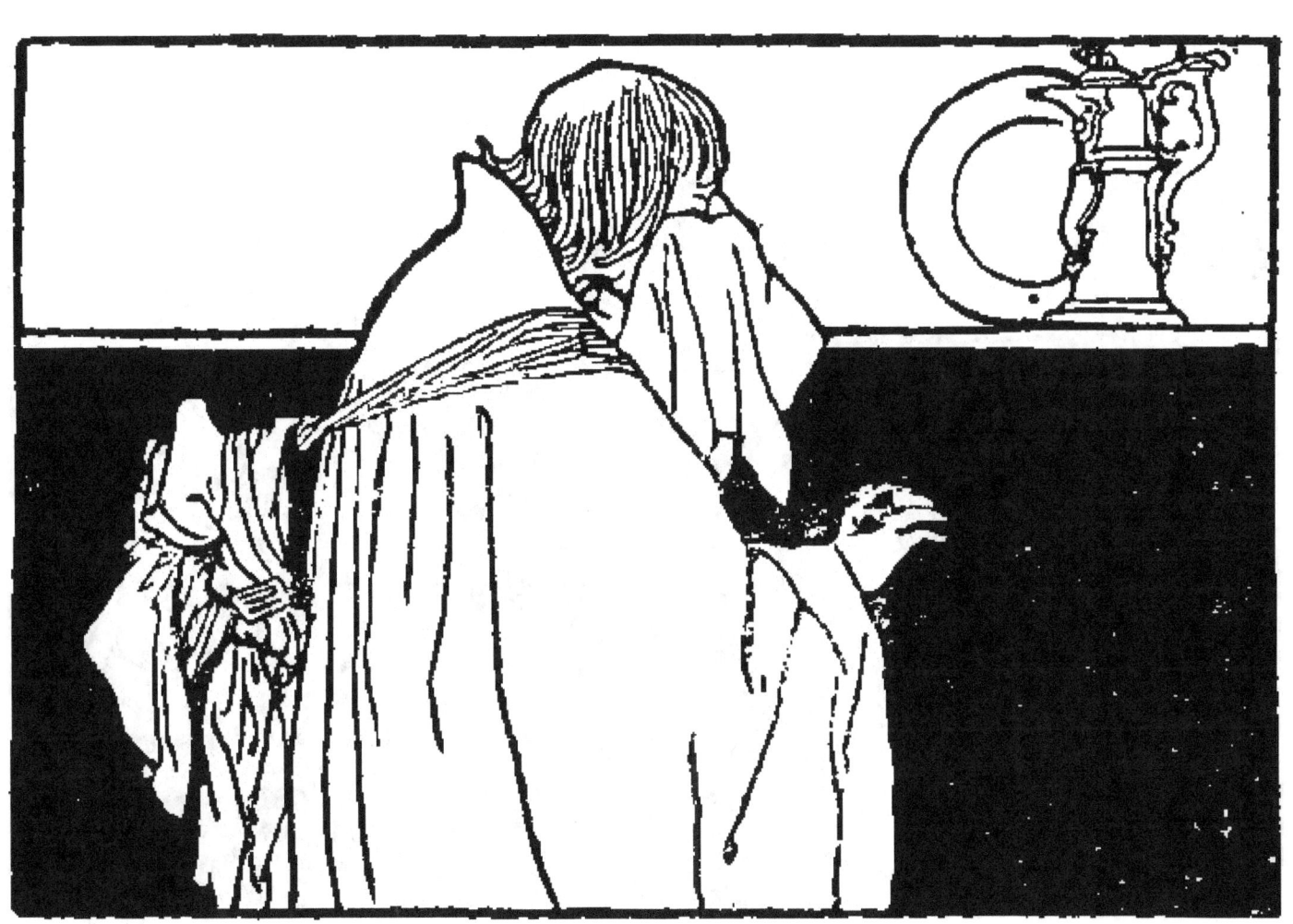

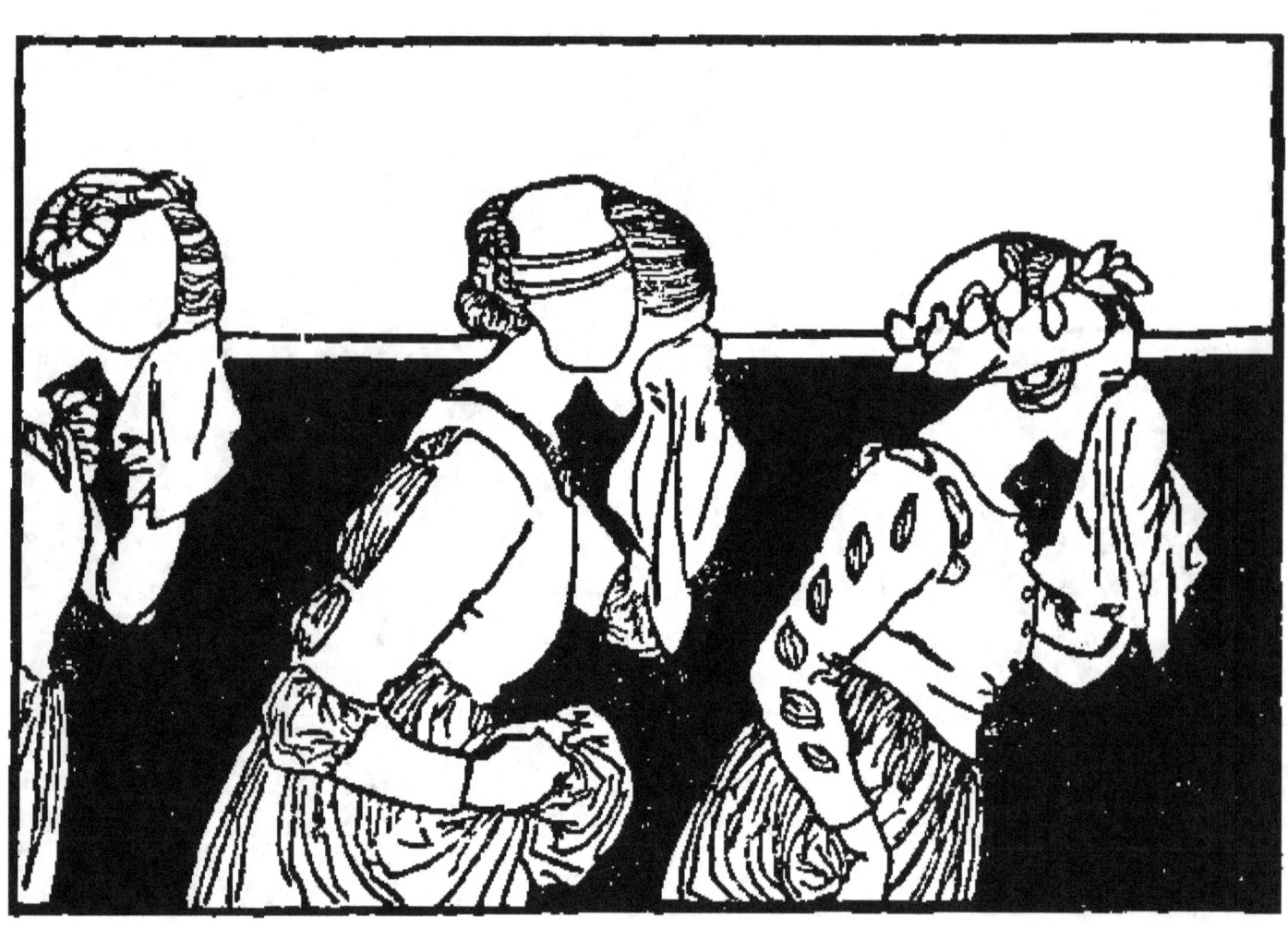

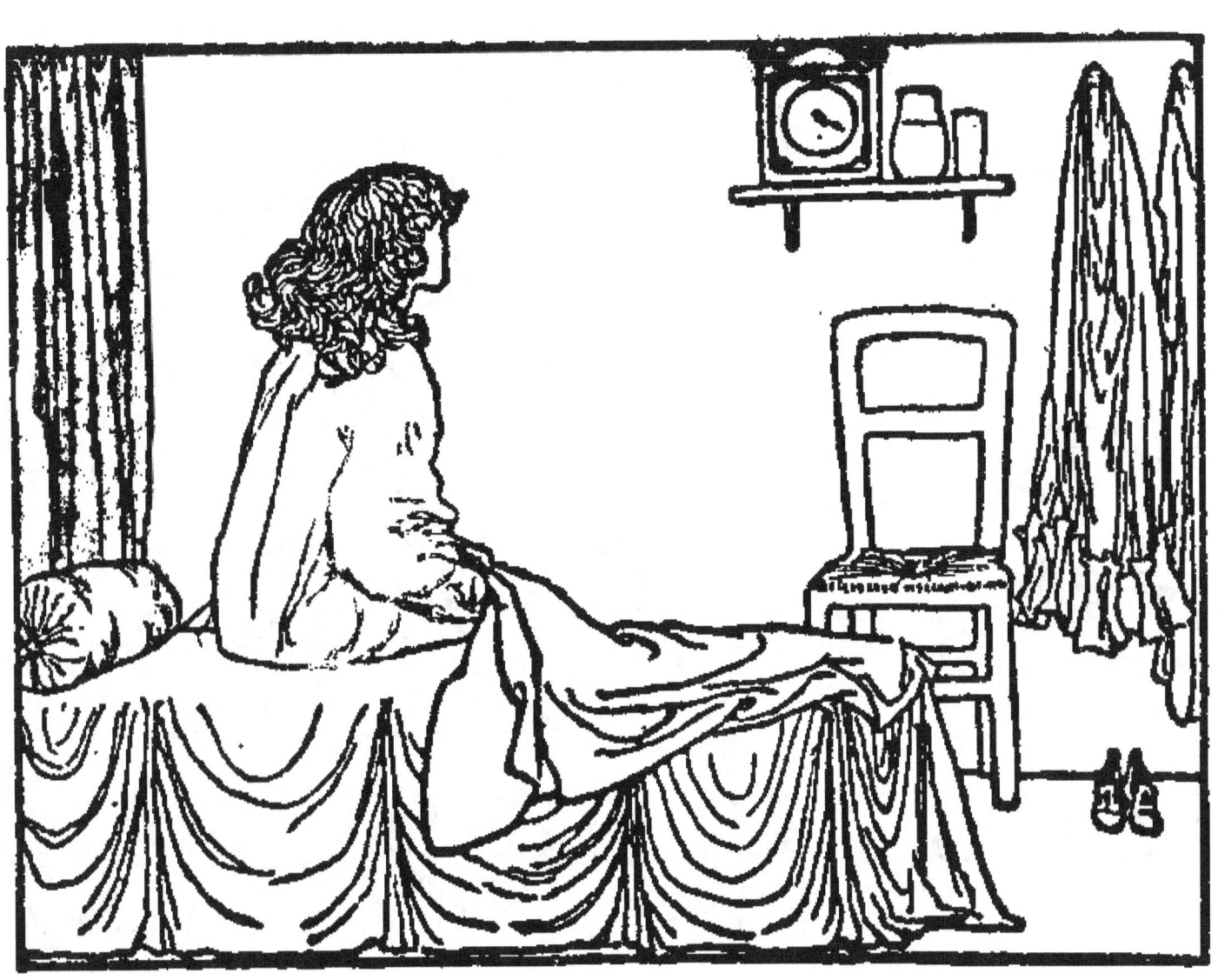

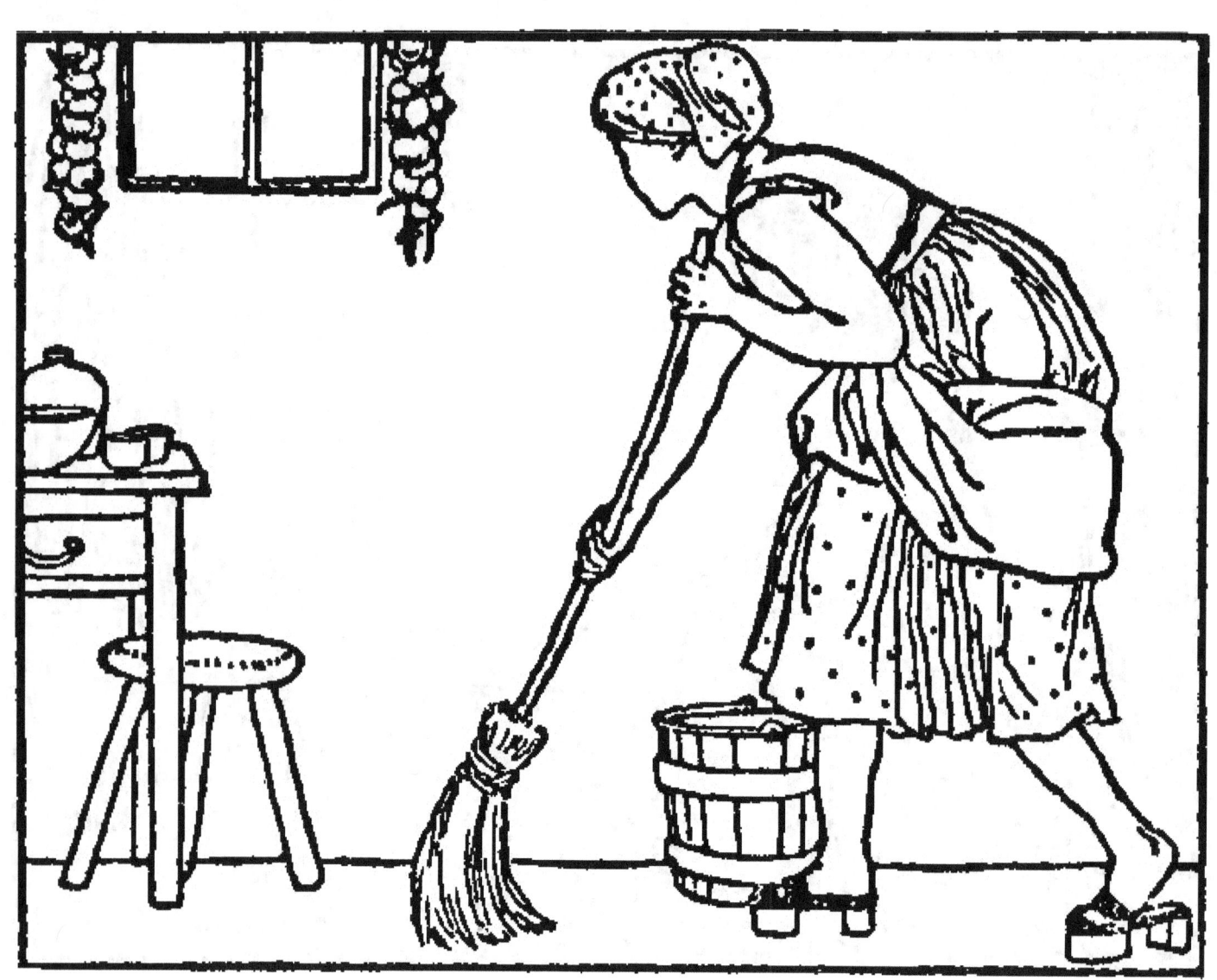

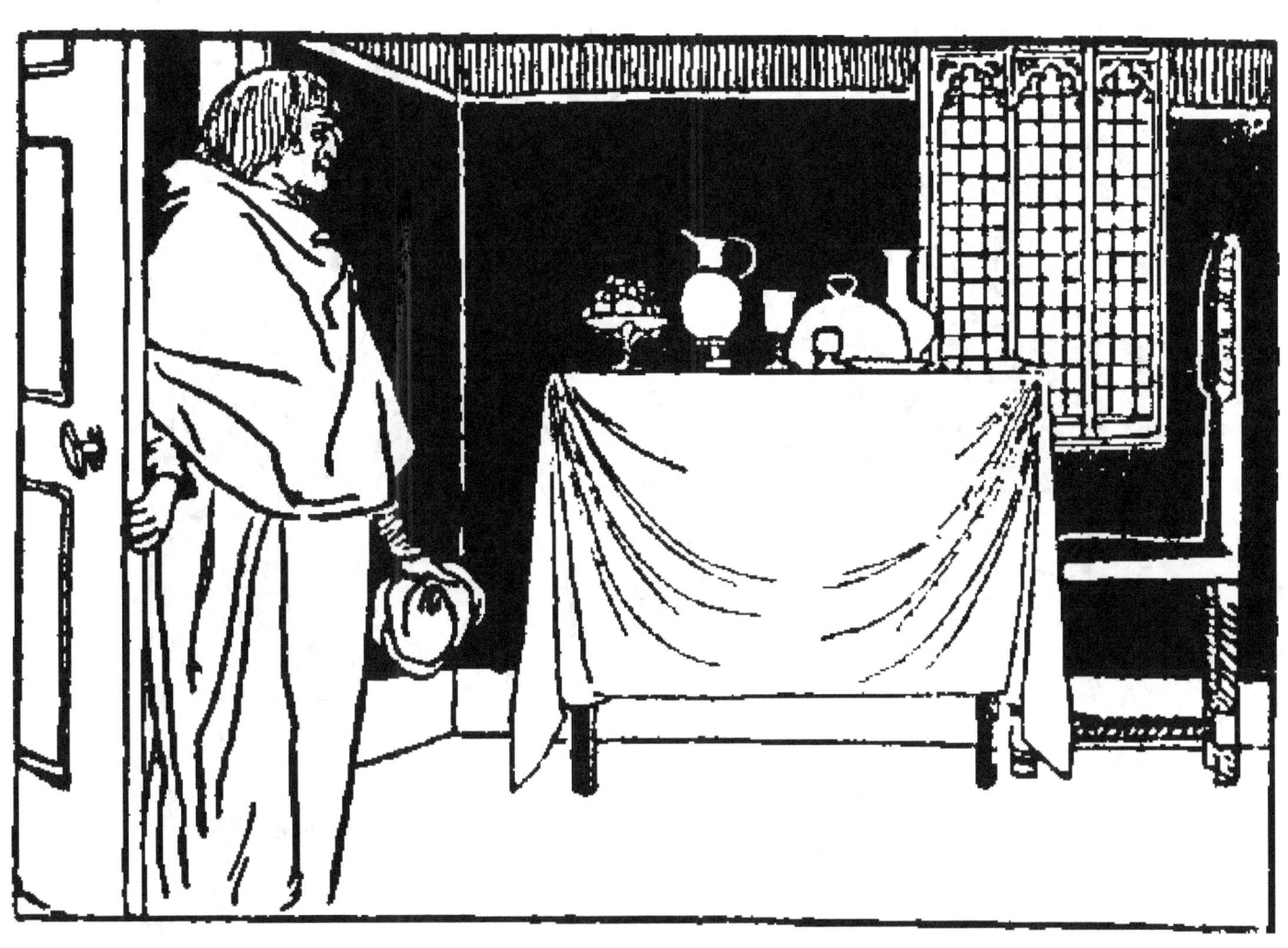

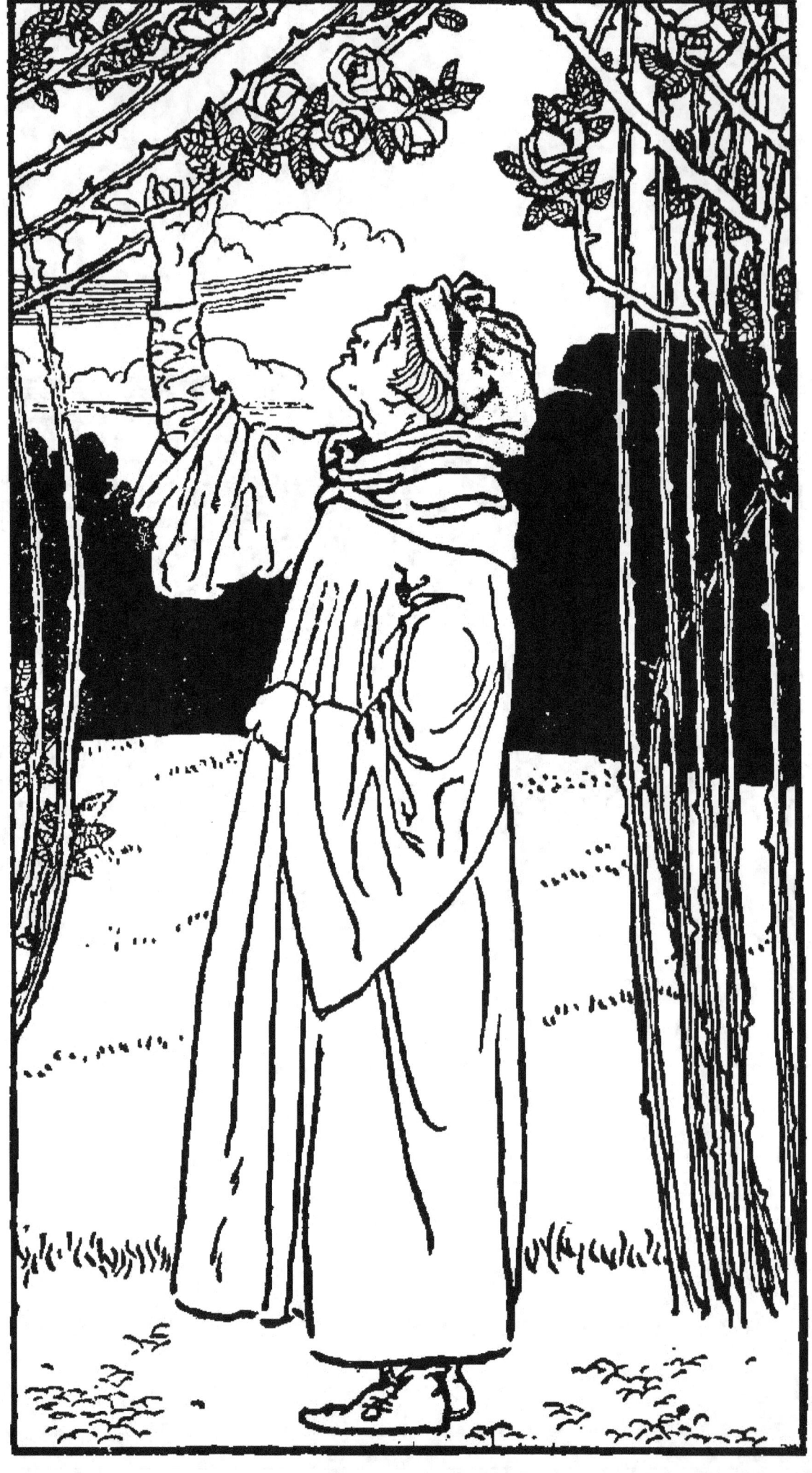

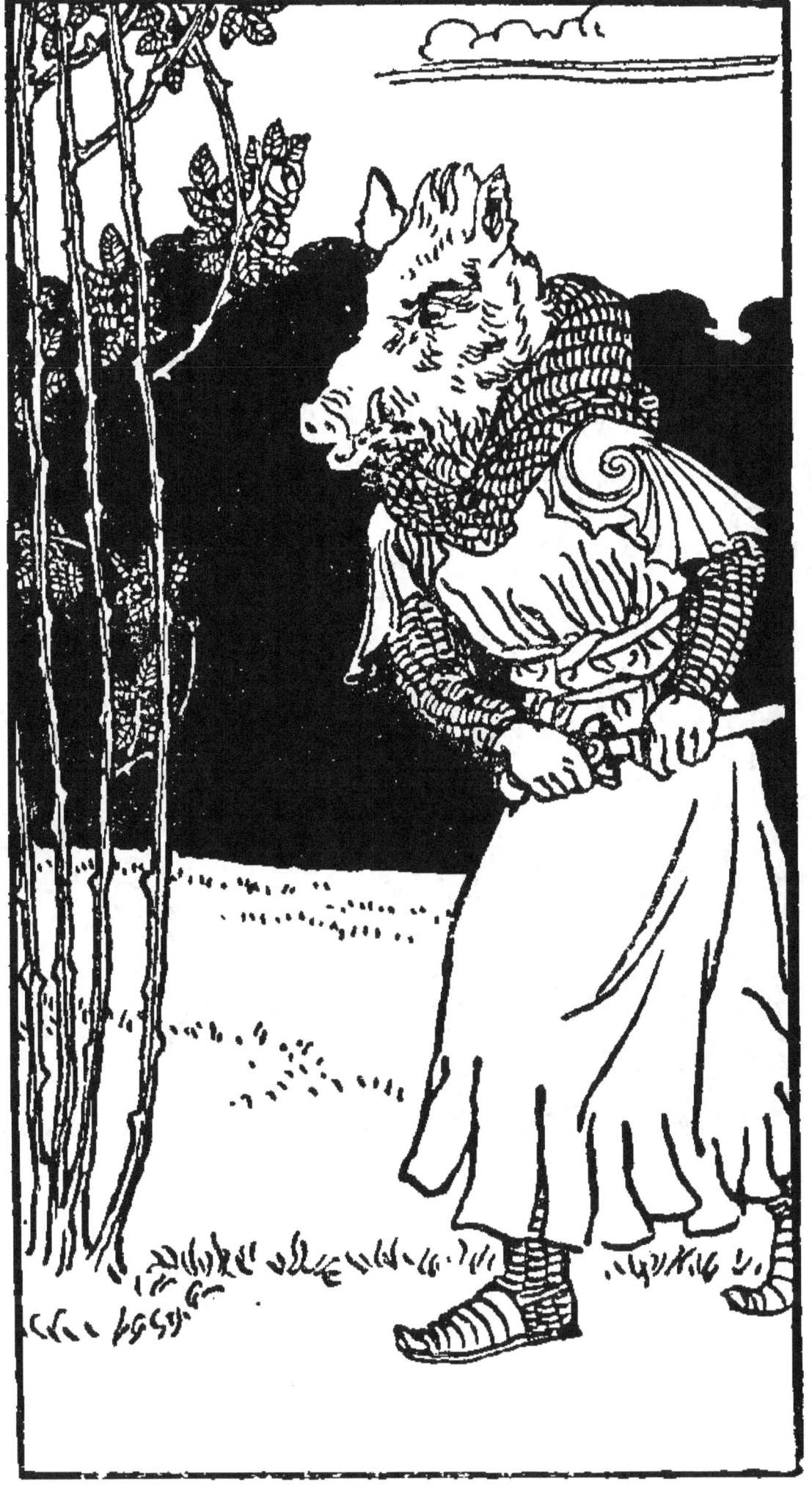

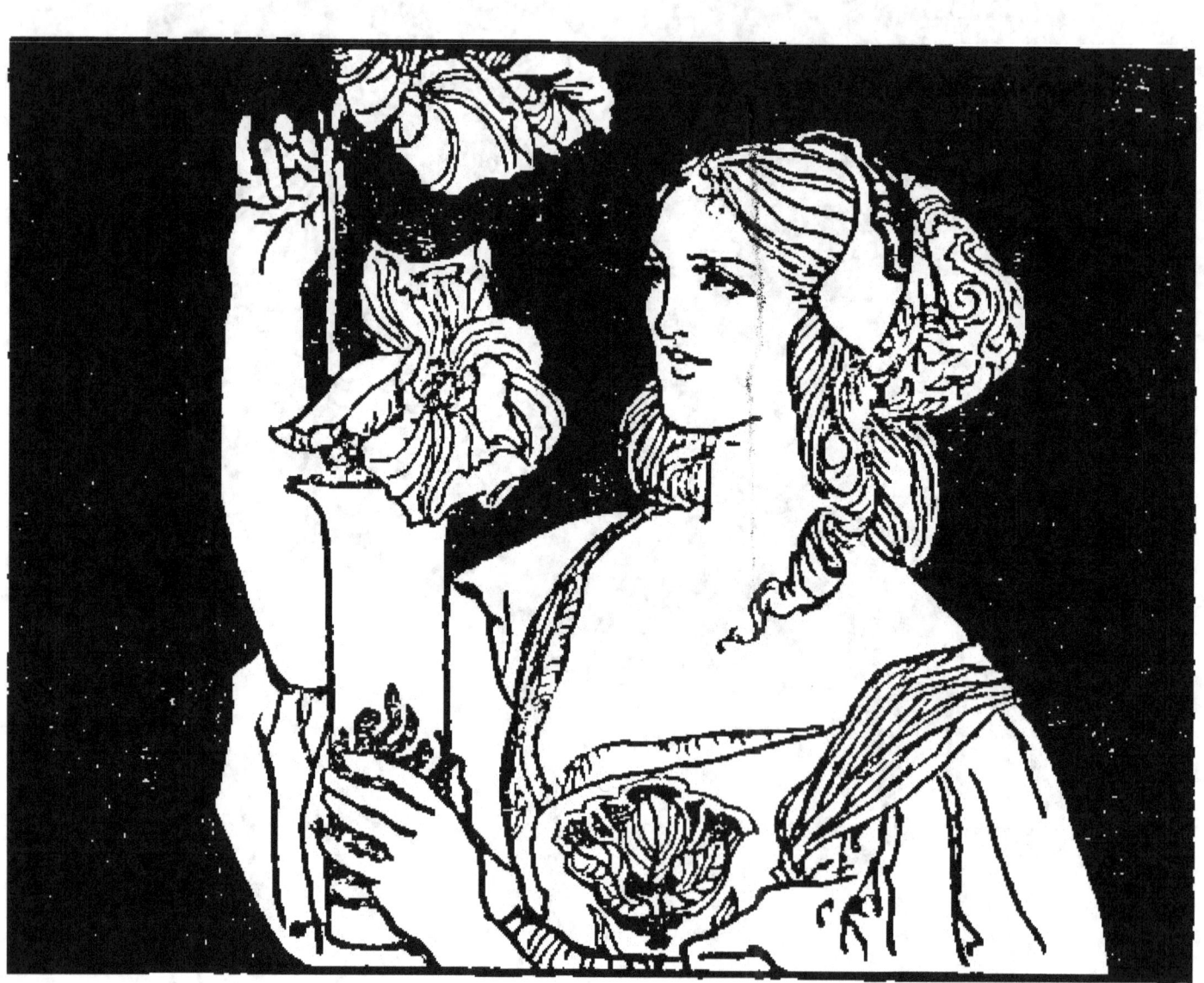

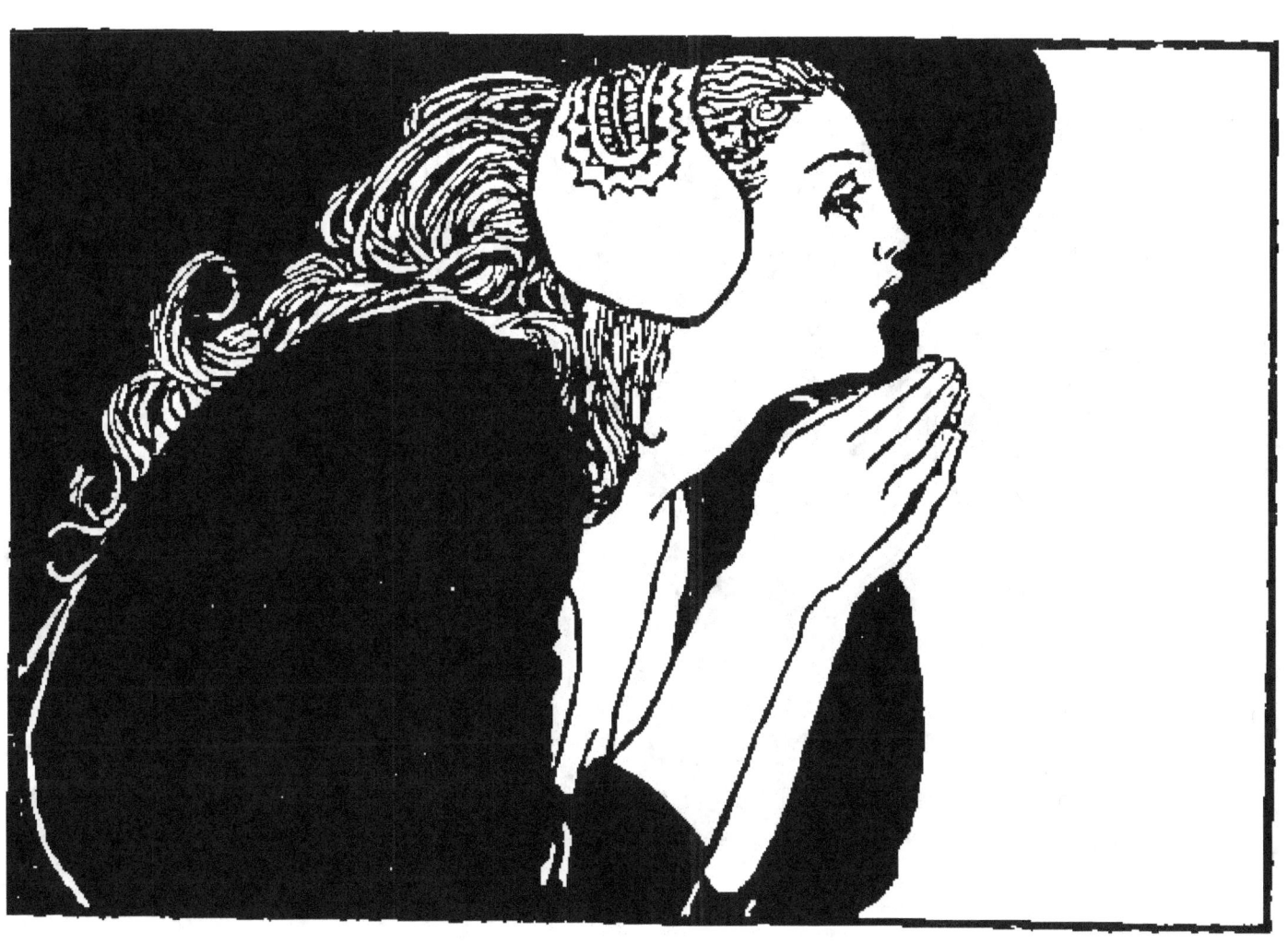

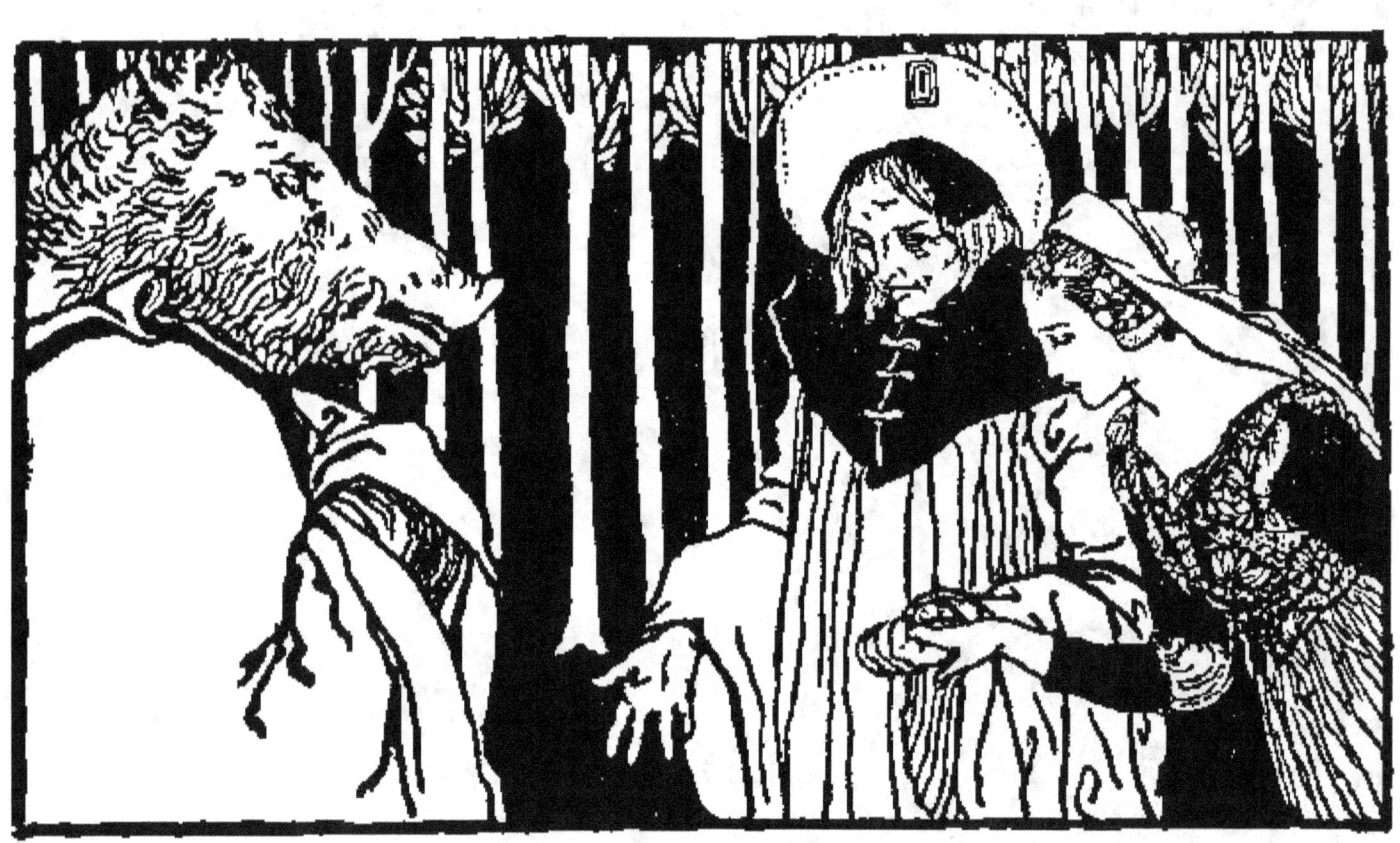

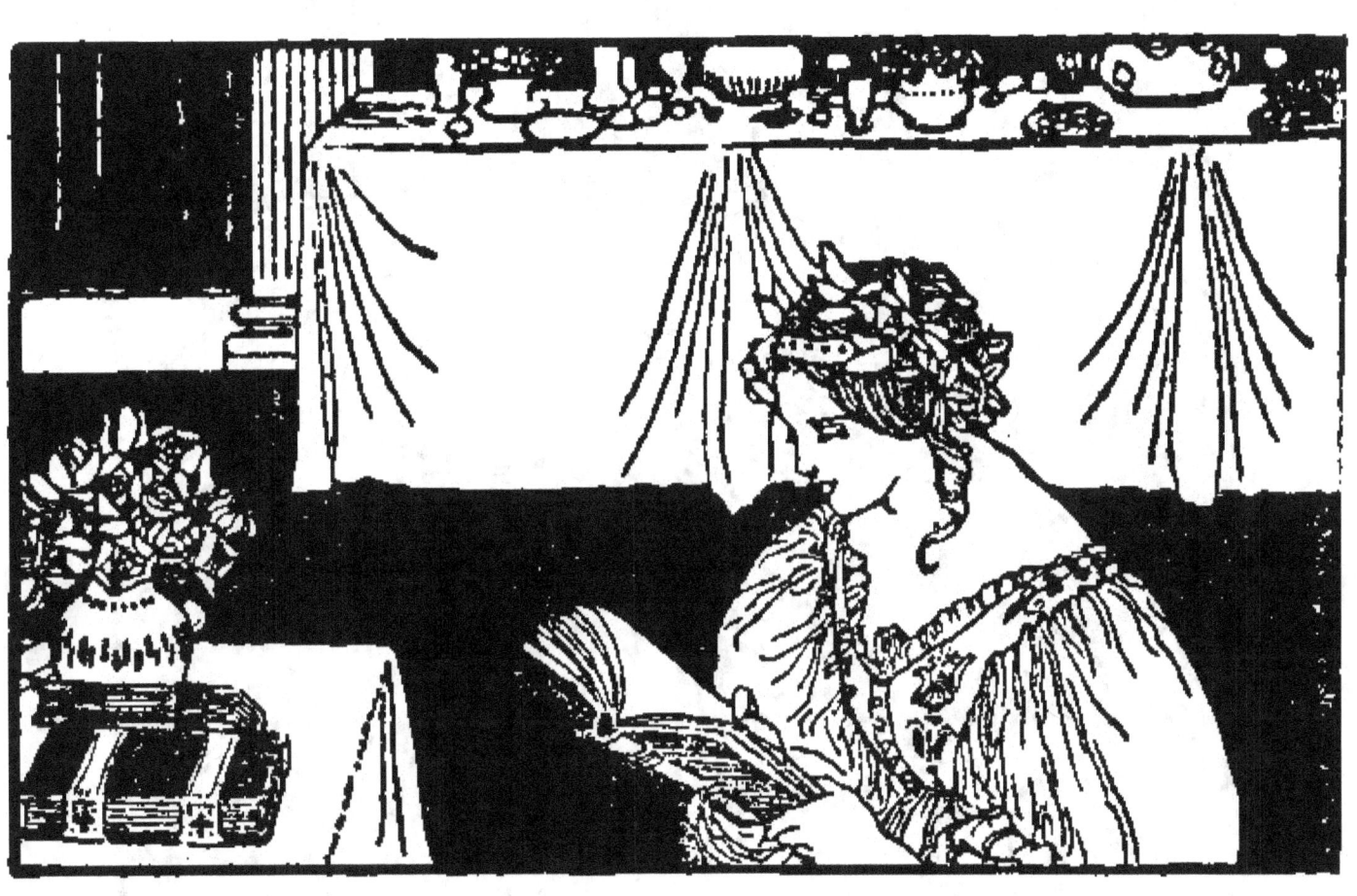

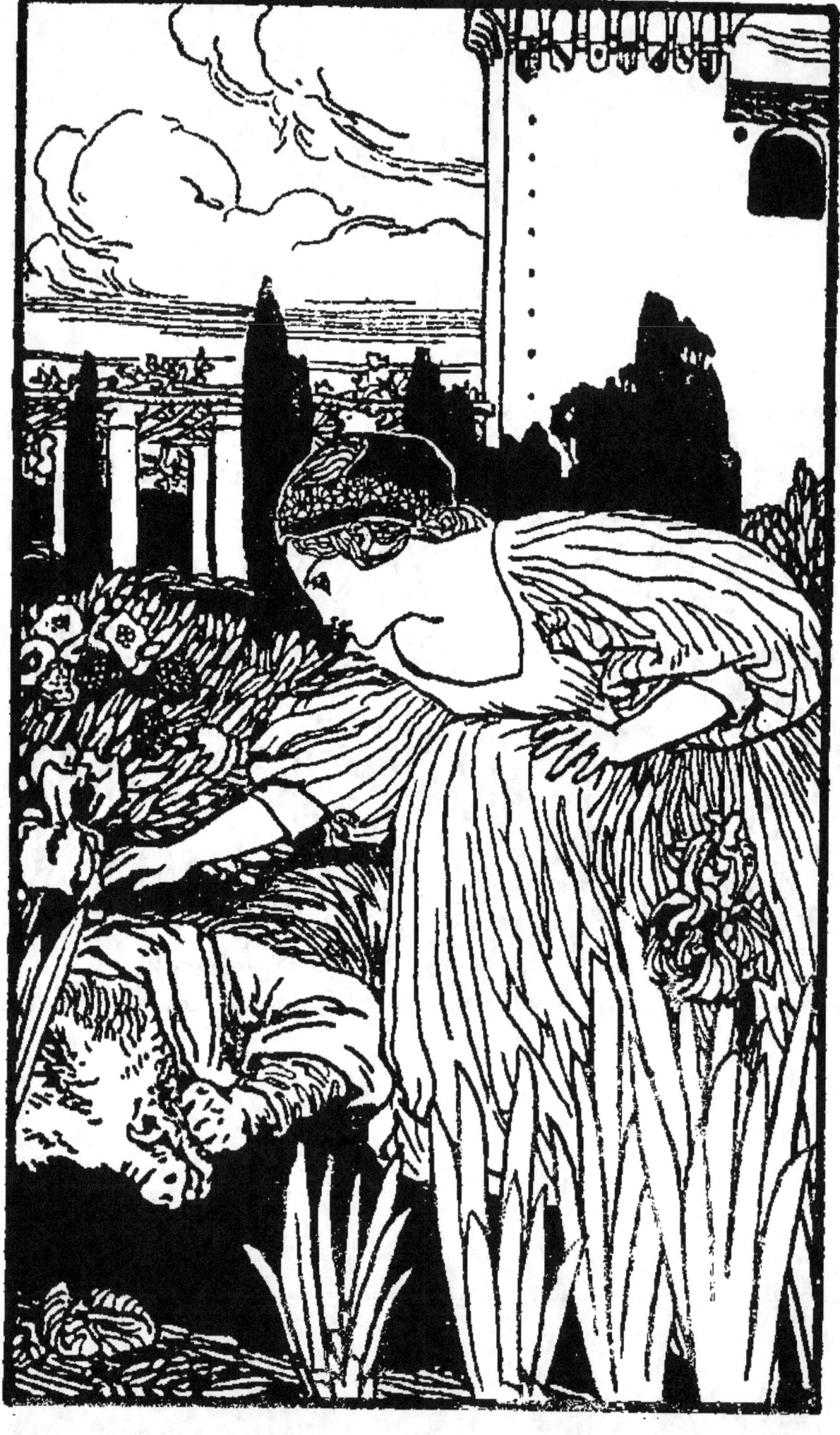

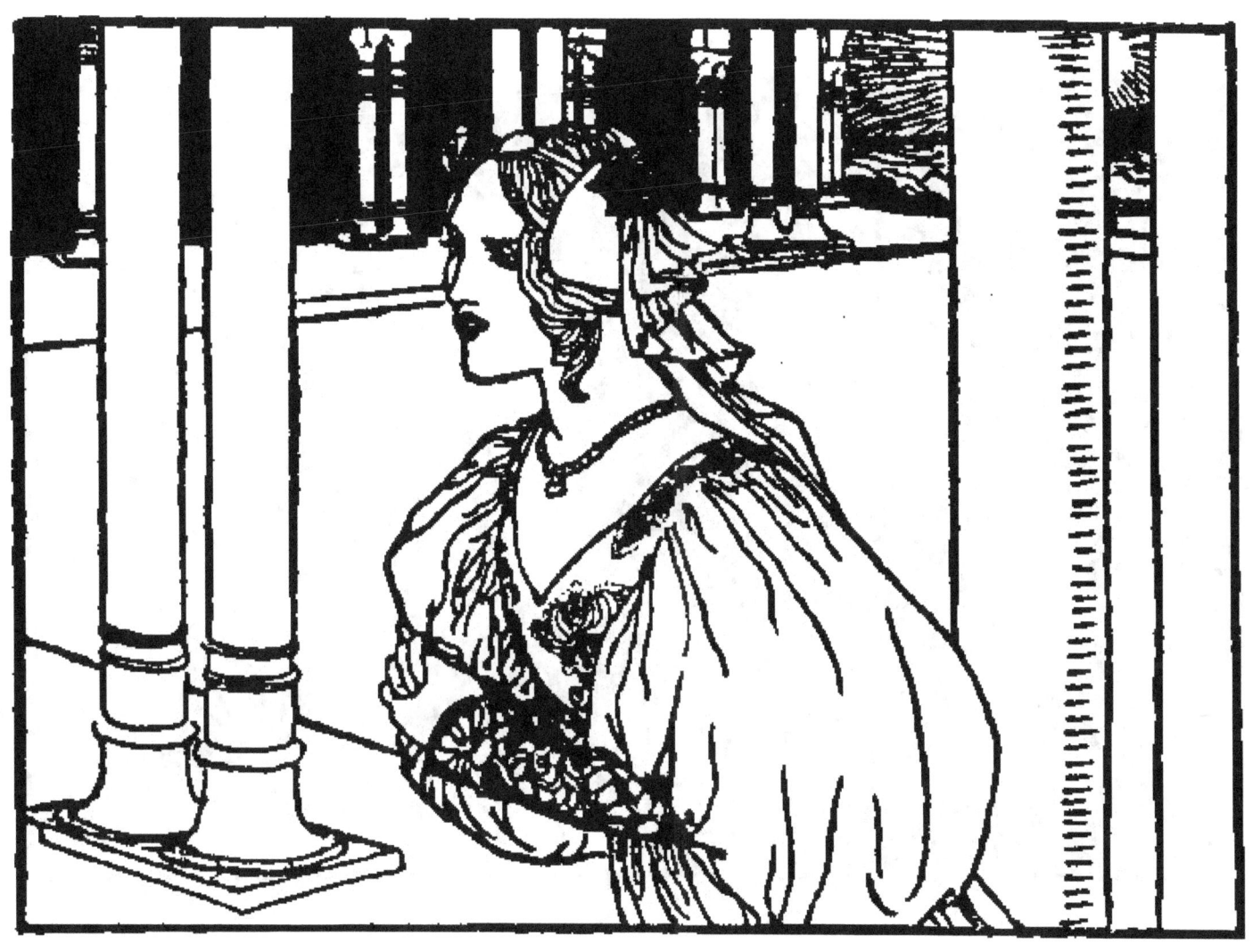

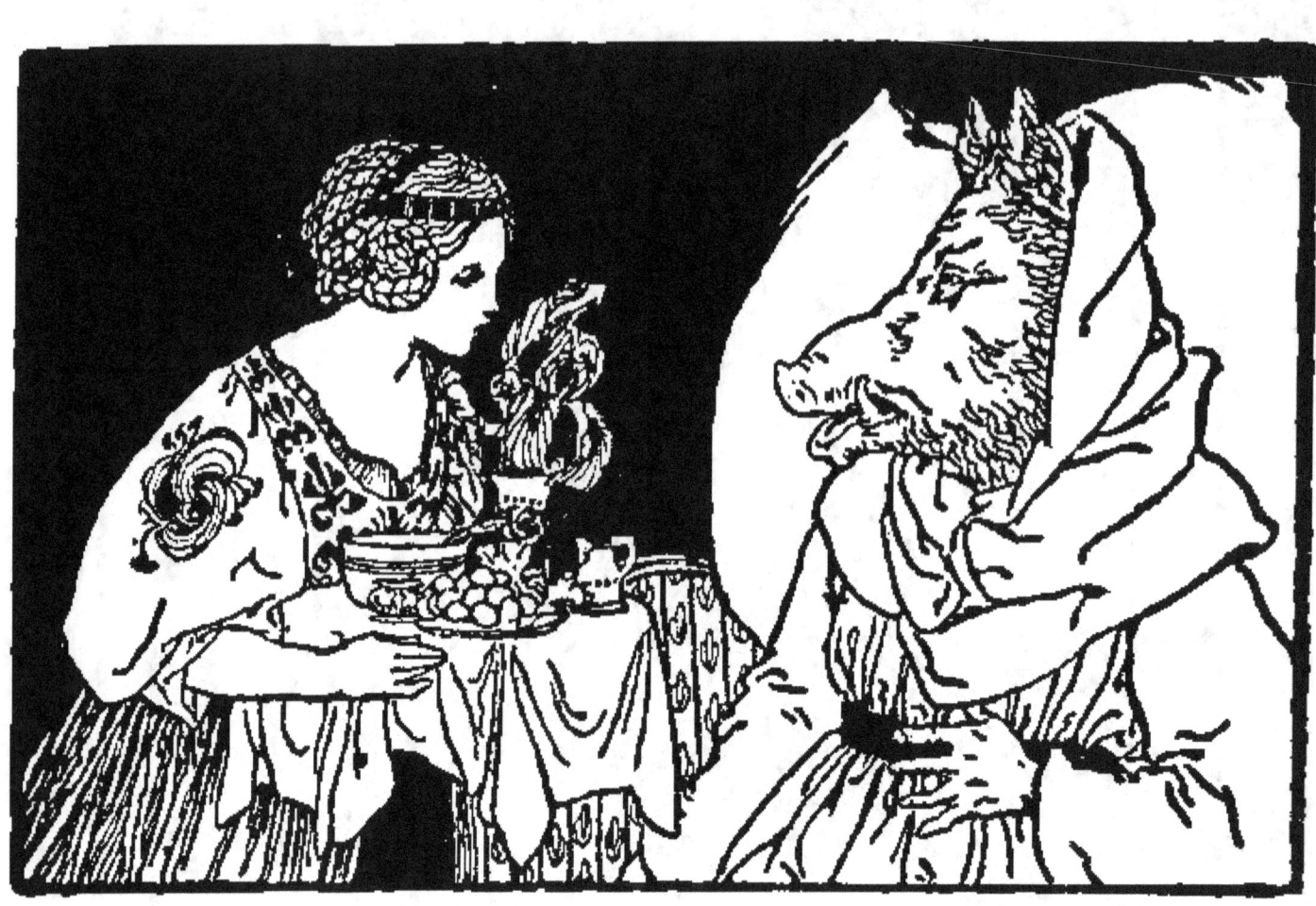

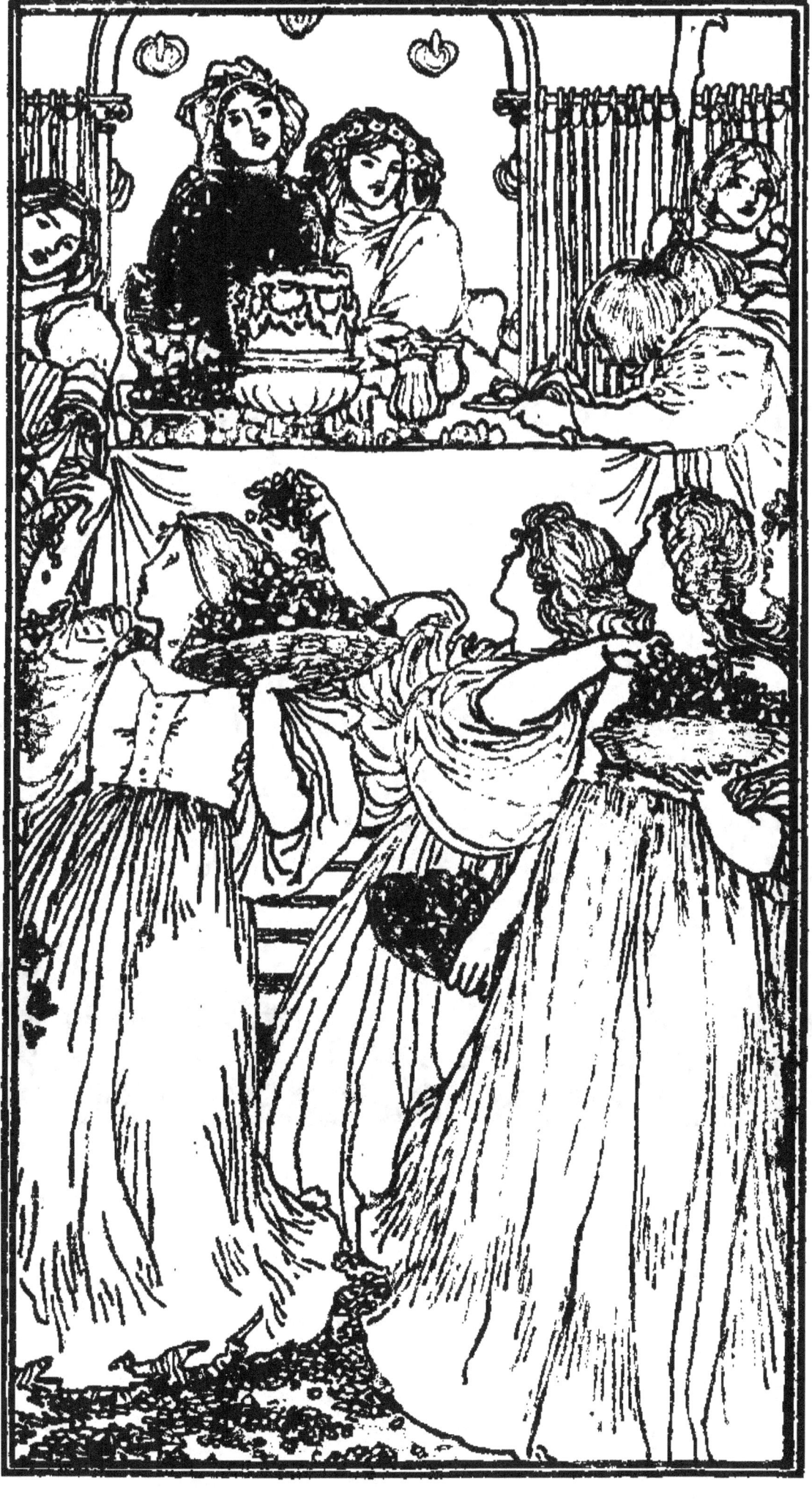

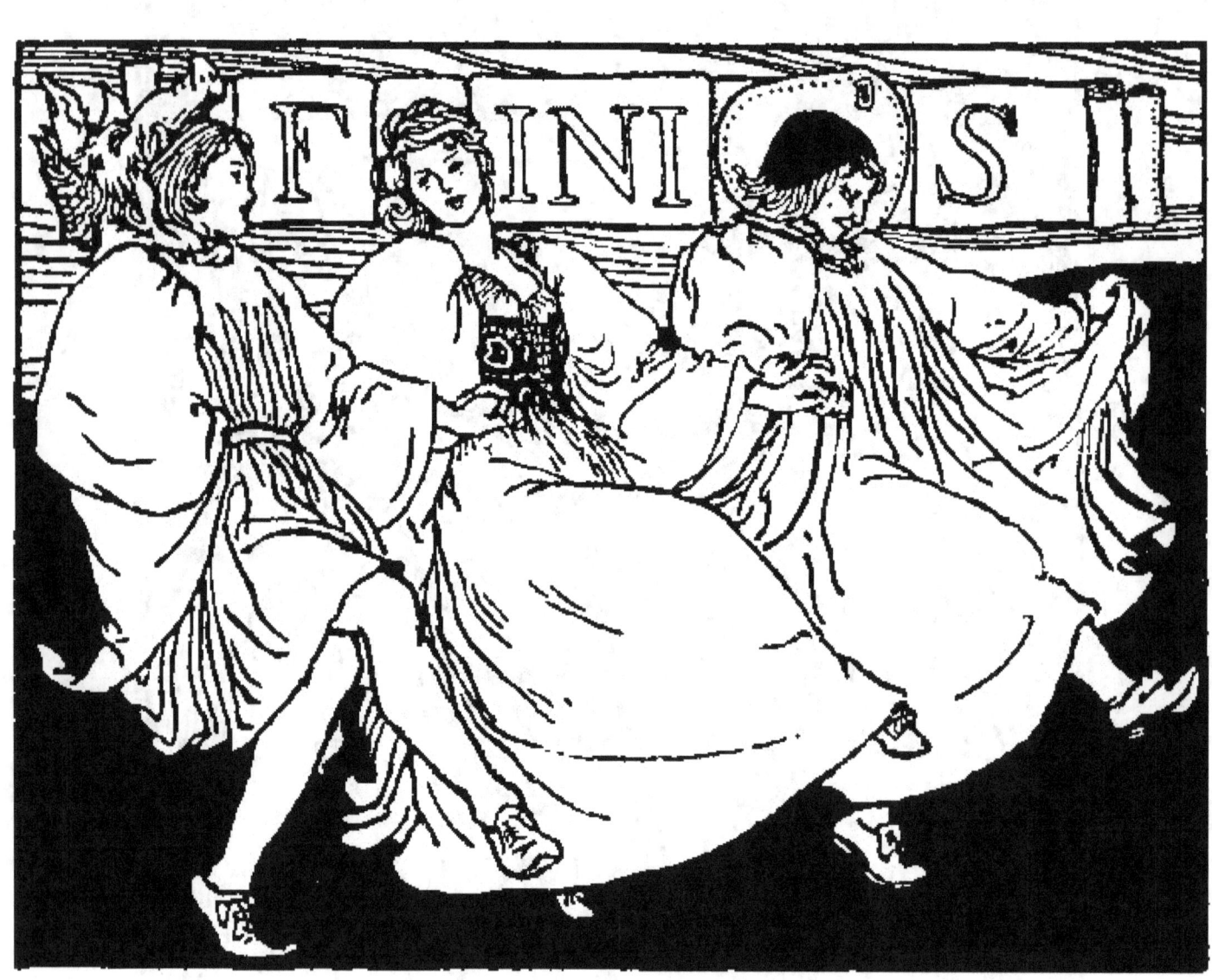

www.ingramcontent.com/pod-product-compliance
Lightning Source LLC
Chambersburg PA
CBHW082216220526
45470CB00010B/3198